Praise for Parents First

"This book is a must for every parent - and grandparent - who wants some down-to-earth, practical advice on helping children to learn, to think, and to use their imagination. It is packed with suggestions. But it is also written with a touch of humour and makes the reader think, as well as the child: I am still trying to work out how the detective knew who killed the lady!"

Lord Ronald Dearing, Education Adviser

"Research shows that support from parents is the single most important driver for pupils' success at school. We don't know *what* people may need to learn in the future but if children are motivated and understand *how* to learn, they will be well-equipped to deal with whatever life holds for them. This book will help parents to support their children in learning how to learn and developing as confident, successful lifelong learners."

Susie Parsons, Chief Executive, Campaign for Learning

"I wish there had been a book like this when my children were young!

"*Parents First* gives you all the guidance you need to help your child become a successful and happy learner. It's full of practical tips and easy-to-use suggestions for: improving self-esteem, confidence and intelligence; thinking clearly and creatively; tackling tasks; answering questions well; encouraging good memorising and spelling habits; and passing tests and exams.

"But there's more! Kay and Garry explain how children learn. They help you to recognise your son's or daughter's unique talents and learning style and they tell you exactly what your child's brain needs to function fully.

"*Parents First* is exciting, but it's also challenging. It asks you to rethink some of your own habits such as listening to your child, admitting you don't know, asking open questions, and praising more than criticising. It describes the kind of life-style at home that will lay the foundations for success at school. And it sets out the steps that lead to a positive and supportive relationship with your son or daughter, even in those tricky moments - like when their bedroom is untidy ... again!

"With its checklists, its down-to-earth activities for the kitchen and car, its helpful hints and its useful summaries, *Parents First* is a treasure trove of practical ideas for every parent who wants their child to be a successful and confident learner both at school and at home."

Paul Ginnis, author of *The Teacher's Toolkit*

Parents First
Parents and Children Learning Together

Garry Burnett and Kay Jarvis

Crown House Publishing
www.crownhouse.co.uk

First published by

Crown House Publishing Ltd
Crown Buildings, Bancyfelin, Carmarthen, Wales, SA33 5ND, UK
www.crownhouse.co.uk

and

Crown House Publishing Ltd
P.O. Box 2223, Williston, VT 05495-2223, USA
www.CHPUS.com

British Library Cataloguing-in-Publication Data
A catalogue entry for this book is available
from the British Library.

ISBN 1904424139

LCCN 2003104688

Printed and bound in the UK by
Cromwell Press Ltd
Trowbridge
Wiltshire

This book is dedicated …

To my parents, Moyra and Brian, who have given me the encouragement and support throughout my life to believe that I can do what I want to do and the confidence to keep trying …

To my wonderful daughters, Vicki and Rachael, whose love and support continue to light up my life. As a parent I know I've made mistakes, but we've learned from each other and I've watched you grow into two beautiful people who enrich the lives of so many others. I am so very proud of you both and love you dearly …

And to my very special friends, Karen, Lyn, Barbara and partner Stephen, who have helped me through some difficult times with their love, understanding and support. Thank you all so very much.

Kay Jarvis

To my parents Maureen and Dennis, and, the proudest parent I know, my wife Louise. Also to Hollie, Laith, Bethany, Grace and William Burnett. My angels.

Garry Burnett

Contents

Acknowledgments iii
Foreword v
Introduction vii

Part 1 **Thinking About Thinking – Reflections on
How Parents Can Support Learning** 1

Chapter 1 **Developing Confidence and Self-Esteem** 3
What causes success? 3
Coping with "setbacks" – raising expectations.........................10
Magic moments 14

Chapter 2 **Effective Communication** 17
Approaching adolescence 18
Effective listening 19
Relationships and disagreements – win–win 21
Quality questioning 25
Coping with jargon 27
Questions for the teacher! 28

Chapter 3 **The Right Conditions for Learning** 31
An effective learning environment checklist 31

Chapter 4 **Building a Healthier Brain for Learning** 35
Health check for your brain 39
Building a healthy brain – checklist 40

Part 2 **Learning About Learning – Practical Strategies
For Parents to Use** 41

Chapter 5 **Mind Mapping®** 43
Getting started with Mind Mapping® 45
The uses of Mind Maps® 46

Chapter 6 **Learning Styles** 49
"Preferred" learning styles 49
Which is the best learning style? 50
Assess your learning style 51
How can I help my child? 52

Chapter 7	**Multiple Intelligences**	**53**
	Understanding intelligence	53
	What are the "multiple intelligences"?	54
	Using your intelligences to learn	57
Chapter 8	**Solving Problems**	**61**
	Improving your child's thinking skills for learning	61
	What is 'problem-solving?'	61
	What's the problem? Analysis and synthesis	62
	Sequencing – solving problems by putting things in order	72
	Coming up with new ideas – hypothesising	76
	Prioritising – choosing the relevant information	79
	Sifting through text for relevant information	81
	Helping with reading – "DIAL" an answer..............................	82
	Making comparisons	87
	Using problem solving skills in different situations	92
Chapter 9	**Memory and Recall**	**95**
	Why is memory important?	95
	Memory CAM (Chunking Association Mnemonics)	101
	Key principles of making a strong memory	107
	Putting it all into practice	108
	Reflecting on the way you learned	111
Chapter 10	**Help Your Child to Learn to Spell**	**113**
	How to learn to learn to spell	113
Chapter 11	**Summary – Making Learning Effective**	**119**
	Stage 1: Preparation – the frame of mind	119
	Stage 2: Get the information	119
	Stage 3: Explore the information	120
	Stage 4: Make a "memory"	120
	Stage 5: Show that you know	121
	Stage 6: Think about the whole process	121
	Conclusion	121
Appendix		123
Glossary		127
Answers		131
Bibliography		133

Acknowledgments

I'd like to acknowledge and thank the following people, without whom this book wouldn't have been possible:

Garry Burnett, who, along with the Learning Development team at Malet Lambert School, first inspired me with his infectious belief in "Learning to Learn".

The Hull School of Health and Social Care, University of Lincoln, who have funded the research and development of the Parents and Children Working Together Project jointly with City Venture. Especially Don Blackburn for his continuing support and belief in the project and Joe Waller and Christine Sutcliffe, with whom the initial idea of working with parents originated.

I'd like to thank the headteachers of the schools involved in the project for sharing my belief in working in partnership with parents, especially Lynda Cook, who was first to pilot the course and is still very support-ive of the project.

And of course the parents who have made this project so successful and my job a pleasure.

Thank you.

Kay Jarvis

I would like to acknowledge the magnificent, pioneering work of Malet Lambert School's Learning Development group (Louise, Kevin and Ellen) which has inspired not only this book, but everything I do and write in this field.

Garry Burnett

Foreword

Parents are a child's first and enduring teachers. They play a crucial role in helping their children learn. Family learning is a powerful tool for reaching some of the most disadvantaged in our society. It has the potential to reinforce the role of the family and change attitudes to education, helping build strong local communities and widening participation in learning.

DfEE (now the Department for Education and Skills, DfES),
Excellence in Schools, **p.53**

It is a commonly expressed view from local and national politicians that some parents "have little or no interest in their children's education". However, this project began from what is known from research and also from our own experiences in working in local communities and schools – that is that parents are overwhelmingly interested in their children's education. What they may not have is a very positive experience of schools themselves, or they may not know what they can do to help their own children.

This programme arose from fairly unspectacular and commonsense beginnings in collaboration between parents and teachers in Kingston upon Hull and academic staff at the University of Lincoln. The initial idea was that children and parents in schools in Hull should have some experience of the possibilities in higher education, once children have finished the compulsory part of their education.

The first idea was to take children into the university to work with mainly information-technology-based sessions, with parents watching the learning process through one-way mirrors (with the children's consent). The initial programme of visits between schools and university for both children and parents soon developed into a more focused programme for parents. In discussion with parents, it was suggested that they would like to take part in the teaching sessions themselves, and their children wanted to observe them. This proved to be so successful in engaging both parents and children with the processes of learning that it was decided to develop a formally recognised programme of study involving both parents and children, which is based on the belief that parents will be more likely to support and value their children's schooling if they understand the benefits of education personally, through gaining academic credit for their work.

There is little doubt from the evidence that children and parents have gained hugely from the learning experiences in the project. This is also partly due to the enormous enthusiasm of Kay and Garry, who have both invested a significant degree of effort and commitment in the programme. This is also visible in the materials that they have developed. However, rather than flattery from me, I think that the test for them lies in the responses of both children and parents to the opportunities for *learning about learning* that are present in these materials.

The experience of the project completely undermines the view that there is a high level of parental apathy about learning. Quite the reverse: there is a clear need to develop more programmes of this kind that satisfy the significant levels of interest that parents have in their children and the process of learning.

Best wishes in using these materials, and we hope that you get as much pleasure from the process as we have.

Don Blackburn
Head of the Hull School of Health and Social Care
University of Lincoln

Introduction

What do you want for your child?

A study done on mothers around the world asked the question, "What do you want your child to be when they grow up?" Mothers in Japan almost always answered, "to be *successful.*"... When American mothers were asked exactly the same question, you can imagine what the answer was: "We want our children to be *happy!*" I was raised in an old-fashioned Italian family. I don't think my father really cared whether I was happy. Oh, I suppose it was of concern to him, and I'm sure that he also wanted me to be successful. But if you had asked my father, and especially my mother, "What do you want your son to be when he grows up?" both would have answered, "We want him to be *good.*"

Tony Campolo, *Let Me Tell You a Story* (2000)

When asked this question, it is very likely that one of *your* responses will be, "For my child to be successful". Without a good education a child's life choices are limited and, naturally, most parents are anxious that their children will achieve their fullest potential.

But many well-meaning parents feel frustrated because they don't know how or where to begin to help them to do so!

We believe that parents and carers are the key to raising aspirations and educational achievement in their children.

You *can* and *do* make a difference!

For most parents their understanding of the education system is based on their own experience of schooldays and, for many, these weren't always "the best years of their lives". Many remember the negative experiences more quickly than they remember the positive!

School experiences may vary from person to person, but one thing is consistent – teaching and learning methods have changed over the years.

The purpose of this book

Parents First: Parents and Children Learning Together aims to explore *how* to learn effectively in order to enable you to develop a deeper understanding of how to support your children with confidence through their school years, and especially through times when they are faced with the challenge of learning in new environments when methods – and expectations of them – may not be as familiar as they were previously.

Natural-born learners?

The range of skills and knowledge you have already taught your child is likely to be extensive. The important point is that *you* were your child's first teacher and have taught them so much already. This need not change during their time at school. Parents have so much to offer in supporting and encouraging their children in "lifelong learning".

A home that nurtures a learning culture teaches children that education is important and is to be valued. We hope that the following exercises and information will equip you with the confidence, skills and understanding you need to help your children to succeed and to develop a dynamic learning culture in the home.

! **Remember:** You were your child's first teacher and have taught them so much already!

So what is "Learning to Learn"?

Parents First: Parents and Children Learning Together is a book designed to improve your child's self-esteem and self-motivation in order that they might feel confident to take on new challenges. It is also about understanding and applying a little of the current research into how the human brain and mind work and to learn ways to "reflect" on *how* we learn effectively. It explains effective strategies for improving memory, for developing our intelligence (of which there are several different types) and for sharpening up thinking skills for learning, answering questions and preparing for examinations. It also explains how we might improve our own abilities to learn more effectively.

We hope that this book will interest and involve you in the learning process and provide you with the skills needed to help your child learn confidently and effectively. In organisational terms the book is very much made up of two halves, the first part looking at and reflecting on past and current learning experiences and the second part offering practical strategies for supporting your child with their learning. The book provides plenty of advice and activities to help you and your child learn to learn and put our ideas into practice. Each tip or activity is indicated by one of three symbols defined below:

 Every time you see this symbol it means that there is an activity you may complete yourself or with your child.

 Next to this symbol you will see words of advice, quotes or slogans.

 This symbol is placed next to advice which is rooted in modern brain research and is designed to allow your child to learn more effectively and naturally.

 ! Remember: If you demonstrate to your child that education matters to you then she will grow up believing it is important for her!

 "After completing the 'Learning to Learn' course, I've a more positive approach about things in general and patience with my children. I now know that my input *can* make a difference to their success."

John Wilkinson (2002), parent of two teenagers

So how do I begin to help?

A question that parents often ask is, "How do I help my child with homework when so much has changed since my own schooldays?" You don't have to know everything to begin helping your child, just to be practical.

It takes confidence to say to a child, "I don't know", because as adults we often feel we should know. It is important to accept that we don't have to have all the answers but we do need to know how to help our children to find out.

! Remember: Always respond to questions from children or they may learn to stop asking!

"Whether you think you can or you think you can't, you're probably right!"

Henry Ford

Parents First: Parents and Children Learning Together will help you to support your child in all stages of the learning process and equip you with valuable insight into how to learn effectively, for life.

A parent's view: "'Learning to Learn' gave me the confidence to realise that I had the ability not only to learn myself, but to help and support my children in a positive way. Their confidence and self-esteem has grown so much that we now enjoy learning together."

Susan Moon, parent of four children

Part 1

Thinking About Thinking – Reflections on How Parents Can Support Learning

Chapter 1

Developing Confidence and Self-Esteem

What causes success?

Have you ever been anxious (perhaps overanxious) that your child should "get it right"? What have been the consequences?

Children desperately want to please adults and love the praise and attention that success brings, but they also try to avoid disappointing them! If a child experiences negative feedback from the parent, he will inevitably start to hide his setbacks and limit his "risk-taking", which in turn can have a negative effect on his self-esteem.

! Remember: Praise all achievements, not just the academic ones!

Every child has strengths (as you will see in Chapter 7 on Multiple Intelligences). As a parent, you should explore with your children their different aptitudes and always praise their efforts. One way you can help to support and maximise learning potential is to create the right environment for learning in the home.

In order to help and support your child to learn you need to understand how to learn effectively and be aware of some of the key factors that enable successful learning. Let us look at this process in more detail.

Think of something that you have learned successfully. Try also to remember the factors that led to your success. Some parents' examples are listed on page 131.

(continued)

Something you learned successfully	Reasons for success

Perhaps it was something you *wanted* to learn and was important or enjoyable for you. It may have been fun, interesting or relevant to your job or your life (driving is a good example). You may have had an inspirational or well-organised and enthusiastic teacher.

Now write down something that you experienced difficulty learning and why.

Something you experienced difficulty in learning	Reasons for difficulty

Why do you think it was difficult? Parents often cite examples from their schooldays when they were asked to recall something they had difficulty learning. It may have been that you found the task difficult to understand, or even boring. Perhaps, in your past experience, you witnessed others being ridiculed, or put down, for asking questions to which they should have known the answers.

"At the school I went to there was only one way of learning and, if you didn't learn that way, you were left behind."

Stan Oliver, parent

"A teacher told me I was thick and would never achieve anything. I now know I *can*!"
Christina Sanderson, mother of five children

4

Think for a moment about a teacher who taught you well. What did she do to help you to learn?

A *good* teacher most probably possessed some of the following qualities. She was enthusiastic, made learning fun, conveyed enjoyment of the subject, communicated effectively, encouraged and supported you, had high expectations and gave informative feedback. Where the opposite is true, learning can be difficult, irritating and hard work!

"I remember my art teacher, Mr Maddison, he was one of the few teachers at that time [1970s] who treated you as an equal by showing respect for young people."
Lyn Dusher, parent

! Remember: Learning should be fun!

Chapter 6 on Learning Styles may help you identify how you prefer to learn, but it is important to note that there may have been a mismatch between how you were taught and the style in which you prefer to learn.

Think about and write down something that your child has learned well in the past (for parents' examples, refer to page 131).

Something your child has learned well in the past	Reasons for success

Why do you remember this event so well? How did you feel when your child achieved her goal? You probably remember feeling very proud when she achieved success. Remember those "first steps" or the time when she was able to ride a bicycle without the stabilisers?

"I remember standing clapping and cheering when my son began to swim. I felt so very proud of him."

Karen Ablett, parent of Thomas

Childhood is full of wonderful moments that we look back on fondly and cherish. No doubt at special times when your children made memorable achievements, you were there to support, encourage and praise them at every step of the way. When children are in their early, formative years we tend to praise and encourage them more openly.

Throughout this time parents use exaggerated praise and facial expressions to demonstrate their pleasure in the child's achievements, which the child responds to positively. As children grow older the tendency to praise openly becomes less frequent, as does the willingness by the child to accept and sanction praise publicly.

Think about the last time someone praised *you* for your efforts.

When was this?

_____

_____

How did it make you feel?

_____

_____

Record how many times in one day you praise or scold your child.

Praise
E.g. for making the bed without being asked.

_____

Scold
E.g. for the state of your child's bedroom.

_____

If you find that you scold more than you praise, take some comfort that, for now, you are in the majority. Parents are often surprised to learn that they do this.

As children discover and exert their personalities, we often find ourselves responding negatively to their inappropriate or inconsiderate behaviour. For many, adolescence is often regarded as a "testing" time for parents and children. Yet, if one of the expectations we have for our children is that they become independent adults who can stand up for what they believe in, then we must occasionally expect our thoughts and opinions to be challenged.

Everyone likes to be praised for his or her efforts. Therefore, it is very important that we be aware of the impact that praising children has on their development. As parents, we need to ensure that we build confidence and self-esteem. Crucially, we need to encourage children to believe in themselves, as well as to equip them to cope with setbacks. They need to believe that everything they aspire to achieve is possible.

PEOPLE WITH HIGH SELF-ESTEEM...
- appear calm and relaxed, even when under pressure
- seem energetic and purposeful
- are enthusiastic about most things they do
- are positive and optimistic about the future
- see minor setbacks as learning experiences leading to success
- are independent and do not need others' approval
- work well with other people, sharing leadership and responsibility
- stand up for themselves and others to reach a fair conclusion
- reflect on their strengths and weaknesses in a constant search for improvement
- set realistic goals.

"If you have high expectations for yourself, high self-esteem and the belief that you will succeed, you will have high achievement. Think like a winner and you will win."
Bobbie DePorter[1]

---

[1] DePorter, Bobbie, 1992, *Quantum Learning*, Dell Publishing, New York.

"If I could sum up 'Learning to Learn' in one phrase, it's about belief not only in your children but in yourself as well!"

Amanda Read – parent of three boys

Coping with "setbacks" – raising expectations

A vital part of the learning process involves the taking of risks and the making of "mistakes". If children are to develop their potential, they must be challenged and find some tasks difficult. It is important that children learn to deal with setbacks (notice that the word "failure" has been avoided).

Parents have an important role in helping their children to cope with "setbacks". For example, at some stage, your child has probably said something like, "I'm no good at spelling" or "I can't draw" and it may be that you may have tried to reassure him by telling him something along the lines of, "You can't be good at everything." If this is the case, your child may pick up the message that it is *acceptable* to give up trying to succeed at some things.

! Remember: Success comes in cans, not can'ts.

Your intentions might be good, but there is a strong chance that your child may develop the belief that you sometimes *expect* him to fail. In the way that many adults invent very creative excuses to explain why they should not do or try things, young people, too, can develop a negative self-image and limit their achievements because they *expect* failure.

It is important to teach your child that to become proficient in any subject or skill, whether it be football skills, maths or playing the guitar, there are times when there will be difficulties to be surmounted. If he equates "difficulty" with "failure", he is likely to give up every time. On the other hand, if you regard a "setback" as an opportunity for learning, the concept of "difficulty" takes on a whole new meaning.

Encourage your child to approach tasks in a variety of ways in order to look for a solution and to think and believe that "Next time I will …"

! Remember: If at first you don't succeed, try a different way!

TIPS FOR IMPROVING YOUR CHILD'S SELF-IMAGE
- Be positive. Tell her you appreciate her efforts.
- Encourage her to believe in her own abilities, e.g. remind her of what she does well.
- Talk openly about your child's qualities.
- Ask your child to tell you the best thing that happened to her today.
- Ask her what she is "looking forward to" tomorrow.
- Praise her at the point she has done something that pleases you – be specific about what it is that you thought was so good.
- Remind your child of a success she achieved despite having difficulties along the way. This helps her realise that setbacks can be overcome.

TRY TO AVOID ...
- focusing on negative situations
- making unfavourable comparisons, e.g. "Your sister would never have done that"
- putting her down or using terms that will make her feel bad about herself such as, "Don't be stupid", "You silly little girl" (try to "love the sinner, not the sin" and let your choice of language reflect that)
- labelling your child, e.g. "You girls are all the same"
- not giving a reasonable explanation, e.g. "You're too young to understand" or "Because I said so"
- being inconsistent in the messages you give, whether in terms of discipline, affection or expectations

If your child does something you disapprove of, try to ensure that she understands what you *expect* from her in the future. Say something like, "The next time, try to ..." or "It would be better if you ..." Self-esteem and confidence cannot simply be acquired overnight. It takes much positive reinforcement and a lot of affirmed successes to make people feel good about themselves.

! Remember: Mistakes are opportunities for learning!

Don't ever think it is too late to improve your own or your child's self-esteem. No one is perfect and all of us can recollect instances when we were made to feel inadequate. But it is how we deal with, and bounce back from, being putdown that is important.

! Remember: Encourage your child to think positively.

Think about hopes and ambitions you had as a child. What did you want to be or do when you grew up? Did anyone ever discount your aspirations as being "silly" or "unrealistic"?

If aspirations are squashed at a young age, invariably the motivation to aspire can become lessened. As we grow up we inevitably revisit and rethink our goals anyway. We do this as we gain a broader vision and acquire more knowledge and life experience.

Children should always be encouraged to have dreams, hopes and aspirations, whatever they are. They need to believe that they can achieve whatever they set out to do. Of course, they will meet with many challenges and setbacks as they go through life and will look to many people for help, support, and encouragement (parents, teachers and family, to name but a few).

"I have tried to open my children's minds to think that anything is possible."
John Wilkinson, father of two teenagers

Did you know that talent often takes time to develop and is not often easily spotted? In *Master it Faster* (1999), Colin Rose writes:

"Walt Disney was fired by a newspaper because 'he lacked good, creative ideas'.

"Einstein could not speak until he was four and could not read until he was seven.

"Beethoven's music teacher told him he was hopeless as a composer."

We can only assume that these creative giants had high self-esteem and self-motivation enough to sustain them and give them the tenacity to carry on.

A SELF-ESTEEM CHECKLIST
How many of the following do you regularly do?

- Tell your child that you like him *because* ... as well as saying, "I love you".

- Listen carefully whenever your child wants to talk to you.

- Show that you're fascinated by your child's abilities and development.

- Tell your child how much he's done to make you feel proud of him.

- Promise unconditionally to care for your child until he is able to cope independently.

- Actively plan for periods of quality time with your child.

- Plan holidays and leisure activities that meet the needs of all the family.

- Teach your child the skills he needs to become a self-sufficient adult.

- Ask for your child's help in a variety of ways/areas.

- Remember to praise and reward for small as well as major achievements.

- Ask for, and listen to, your child's opinion and show respect for views that differ from your own.

- Listen to and support your child in difficult and hurtful times.

- Stand back and allow your child to take risks and make mistakes.

- Say, "I'm sorry" and "I don't know" rather than pretend that you know all the answers.

Magic moments

Positive associations with "personal best" achievements can provide powerful connections in the brain that reinforce self-esteem.

Think about a time when you did something you were really proud of or that made you happy and write it down.

_____

_____

_____

_____

_____

It could be a time when you won a prize for some personal achievement, a family celebration such as a party or get-together or maybe when you were praised for doing something really well.

Now do the same with your child.

_____

_____

_____

_____

_____

It may be a time when your child needed to show courage; it may be when he stood up for himself against someone who was being loud and unfriendly. Maybe it was when he had to go in front of a large group of people and speak or read aloud. Maybe you are thinking of a family holiday or day out, a visit to a concert, the theatre or a school trip.

Choose three favourite magic moments.

Write a description of the time they happened. Try to describe the sights (the colours and surroundings), sounds and feelings you remember. You can use some of the following ideas to help you.

One of my magic moments was when   _____

_____

_____

It was a magic moment because   _____

_____

_____

Another one was when   _____

_____

_____

This was memorable because   _____

_____

_____

My final magic moment was when   _____

_____

_____

This was a magic moment because   _____

_____

_____

Make a "Magic Moments" treasure chest. Take a shoebox or a large envelope and place a selection of these "magic moments" mementoes in.

Use these treasures to remind yourself and your children of the many good things they have already done and achieved.

We all have times like this that we look back on and remember fondly. Many of us keep photographs, certificates, memorabilia such as concert programmes and even ticket stubs or other souvenirs of the happy occasion. Have you noticed how just looking at these mementos can also bring back a flood of positive memories and positive feelings? They make us feel good. We want you to bring this feel-good factor to learning.

In summary

- Reflect on your own successes.
- Remember, it's OK to say, "I don't know but we'll find out together".
- Success is more often achieved when learning is fun, enjoyable and interesting and matched to your own learning style.
- The learner should see relevance in what they are doing and be motivated to succeed.
- Children need praise, support and encouragement to feel their efforts are important and valued.
- Remember their confidence and self-esteem can be fragile.
- Children need to grow with belief in themselves that they can succeed in whatever they want to achieve.
- Be positive.
- You *can* and *will* make a difference.

Chapter 2

Effective Communication

Another crucial element, and part of developing self-esteem and confidence is the ability to communicate effectively. A child who is listened to and whose opinions are respected is more likely to grow up feeling positive and valued. Effective communication is a skill that we nurture in our children from the moment they are born. Most people adapt their behaviour and communication techniques to suit the child's level of understanding.

When your child was very young you probably used "baby talk": you held your child quite close to your face so she could see your eyes and you smiled a lot. Researchers have found that young babies focus on facial expressions and tone of voice. As they develop and begin to speak, we modify our language so that they understand. We tend to keep sentences short or use single words or phrases.

Adults sometimes make the assumption that a child shares the same level of understanding and has the same reference points as they do. But this is not always so!

In *Cider with Rosie* Laurie Lee as recalls his first day at school:

"What's the matter, Loll? Didn't he like it at school then?"

"They never gave me the present!"

"Present? What present?"

"They said they'd give me a present."

"Well now, I'm sure they didn't."

"They did! They said: 'You're Laurie Lee, ain't you? Well, just sit there for the present.' I sat there all day but I never got it. I ain't going back there again!"

Approaching adolescence

Adolescence can be a difficult time for parents and teenagers, as young people begin to assert their independence, take risks and experiment with relationships and lifestyles. To communicate effectively with our children we must first recognise and accept that this phase of their lives will also challenge our own beliefs.

! Remember: As parents we must be ready to accept that our views and thoughts may be challenged by our children. It's part of growing up!

Discuss with your child how you felt about your own relationships with your parents – their grandparents. How would you have liked your own relationship with your parents to have been?

_____

_____

How would you like your relationships with your own adolescents to be?

_____

_____

Are there any similarities or differences?

_____

_____

Discuss these with your child and set out some agreed principles below. For example, 'Talk, don't shout.", "Ask, don't demand.", "Respect each other's views and opinions."

_____

_____

We have agreed that

_____

_____

Effective communication is essential in any kind of relationship – within the home, with family, with friends or professionally. Let's examine the key elements of effective communication more closely.

Effective listening

When communicating with your children, do you "listen" or do you "hear"? When we "hear" we don't closely analyse what is being said or its implications or pay attention to the finer meaning expressed in body language. Have you ever found yourself saying, "uhmm" and "yes" in the appropriate places of a conversation without really listening to what has been said?

Ask a friend or a partner to speak to you for a few minutes about any subject he wants. While he's talking, you remain totally silent. In addition to being silent, try behaving in an inappropriate manner. For example, through your body language, act as if you are bored with his conversation.

What was his response to your actions?

_____

_____

How did you make him feel?

_____

_____

How did you feel?

_____

_____

Did the speaker stop talking because he felt you were being rude or that you weren't listening? Did you feel uncomfortable? You probably made the speaker feel highly uncomfortable and self-conscious too!

May I suggest you apologise immediately!

Listening is about being sensitive to the words, their implicit and explicit meaning and *how* they are expressed. Tone of voice, sensitivity to the pace of speech and body language are all important characteristics of good listening. We listen with our eyes as well as our ears!

! **Remember:** Don't forget to tell your child you enjoy spending time with them!

! **Remember:** Children need to know you are listening attentively to them. It makes them feel valued.

Tips for effective listening

1. Physically face each other and make eye contact
Looking at the speaker shows that you are interested in what is being said. Try not to stare though as too much unwavering eye contact can be intimidating and make the speaker feel uncomfortable! This is crucial with children: they need to know that you are listening attentively to them. Looking away as someone speaks to you can easily destroy her confidence that she has your full attention, and, with it, her willingness to confide in you.

2. Pay attention both to what is being said and how the speaker is saying it
Try to be aware of what the speaker is not saying! Is he relaxed or does he seem to be nervous? Often, children will hint at a problem to gauge your reaction. A child who is being subjected to bullying at school might say a little about an incident or the perpetrator at first, just to see how you respond.

3. Show you are interested and are following the conversation by offering verbal and nonverbal "prompts"
You can do this by nodding or saying "uhmm" or "yes/no" in appropriate places. Similarly, you could ask, "And what happened next?" or "What do you mean?" Another way to demonstrate you are listening attentively is to paraphrase, and repeat part of what has been said: for example "So what you're saying is …"

Have you ever listened to your child read while cooking the evening meal or had a conversation while doing something else such as watching the television? Many parents do! It isn't always convenient for an adult to listen actively when the child wants to speak.

The important point is that, as parents, we should make time to talk with our children, giving them our full attention and trying to ensure we ask productive questions. We will come back to questions and effective questioning later.

Relationships and disagreements – win–win

Do you remember disagreeing with your parents over various issues? How were these disagreements generally resolved? Did your parents end up asserting their authority over you? Did it come down in the end to a case of "I'm the parent and you'll do as you are told"?

Teenagers often feel they are being treated unfairly (remember Harry Enfield's character, Kevin?) and if communication isn't effective then it can all come down to "who has the power"! Being able to resolve conflicts effectively is an important ingredient of being "emotionally intelligent" and an important quality of healthy relationships and understanding between parents and children. There are strategies and structures you can use to help with this process.

! **Remember:** Try to avoid power struggles!

"I now have more patience with my children to sit and explain gently and quietly how to do things. I feel sure we get on a lot better for it."

Carol Whittaker, parent

It is often easier to assert our authority over unreasonable children than it is to discuss things calmly, rationally and logically. Try not to damage a child's confidence by enforcing authority too harshly.

! **Remember:** A young person will build confidence and self-esteem if her views and opinions are listened to and respected. (This doesn't mean to say she should get her own way!)

This is often easier said then done!

Let's take a practical look at how this can be achieved in an all-too-typical everyday situation!

Scenario

Your child's bedroom is a mess. You want it to be tidied up. How can this be resolved?

Options

Perhaps you could try out this role-play with your child. They could be used as a starting point for a discussion about the best way to negotiate how to achieve a 'tidy room'!

The first two examples are ones I've used in the past with my daughters when I've seen the state of the bedroom and have already decided that they can't win!

> **Example 1**
> **Parent:** Your room *IS* tidy isn't it?
> **Child:** Yes
> **Parent:** It *isn't* tidy enough, I've been in there and it's a tip! Go and tidy it now please.
>
> **Example 2**
> **Parent:** Your room *IS* tidy isn't it?
> **Child:** No, not really
> **Parent:** Then it *should* be. Please go and do it now before I go and put everything on the floor in a dustbin liner and tidy it *MY* way!

"If you've got a positive attitude things seem so much easier."
John Wilkinson, father of two teenagers

These examples are obviously negative and non-productive. The child cannot win either way. My responses were driven by my emotions and were not very rational. The child has not been given an opportunity to make choices about when or how they will tidy up their room or been given any peramaters with regards sanctions or consequences should they chose not to tidy their room!

Your child may ask why it has to be tidy at all. They may want you to respect their choice to have their room as they choose!

If faced with this situation then either explain calmly why you want the room to be tidy or why you will respect their choice with regards their personal space.

You could simply ask them to tidy their room. This may work on the first time of asking! But when will they do it? How long will you keep asking? What if it isn't done? What then?

Perhaps you could try the following role-play with your child and discuss the different approaches. Ask your child which would be more successful at achieving the outcome you desire?

> **Parent:** I'd like you to tidy your room please, before tomorrow. I'd like all the clothes picked up off the floor and placed in the laundry basket. At the very least, please make sure your floor is clear.

> **Child:** I'm going out tonight and have homework tomorrow. I'm off to the disco on the following night. I haven't got time.

> **Parent:** I'd like your room tidy before you go to the disco. If the room isn't done by then you won't be allowed to go to the disco. This gives you almost 3 days to fit it in. It's up to you when you do it but please make sure it's done.

Try to ensure you are listening to your child's views and that you are clear about what it is you wish to achieve, what the outcome will be and any consequences should the child not meet with your wishes. Be prepared to be a little flexible but most importantly discuss the matter together calmly and rationally!

A structure for negotiation!

A useful structure for resolving this kind of conflict that shows that you are listening to the views of your child might include some of the following elements:

1. Discuss the issue calmly.
2. Ensure that you both share a common understanding.
3. Negotiate a reasonable timescale.
4. Understand what the outcome will be.
5. Have agreed consequences.

So ...

1. Discuss calmly with the child the fact that you·would like the room tidying.
2. Ensure that you both share a common understanding of what is meant by "tidy" and appreciate each other's needs and concerns.
3. Negotiate a reasonable timescale that is acceptable to you both and make sure that the child understands what the outcome will be if the job isn't done.
4. Agree the consequences should the bedroom not be tidy!

It is important to discuss the task when calm (not when you've just seen the state of the room!). If you can start off calmly you will both be more likely to negotiate and compromise.

 ! Remember: Set out clear expectations and consequences. Negotiate rewards and sanctions.

This approach gives children choices and the feeling of control over their own actions. Whatever the outcome they will be clear about what is expected of them, as they will have negotiated the terms with you. They will also be aware of the consequences if the job isn't done! You may have rewards in mind or you may have agreed on a reasonable sanction until the task is completed. Typically assertive teenagers are never going to like sanctions but it is important for them to learn that actions have consequences. In this situation they have the power to choose the outcome.

Both sides must stick to the agreement. Many parents find it easier to give in, to make life simpler. Children who grow up with inconsistent messages and threats that are not carried out learn very quickly what they can get away with! Disagreements over completion of homework, meeting deadlines or timekeeping might be resolved more easily by using a similar logical pattern to this one.

! Remember: Praise success and support through children's setbacks!

Quality questioning

Whether you want to talk with your child, listen to him read or help with homework, negotiate a time that is convenient for you both and stick to it!

You know your child better than anyone, therefore, you will be able to identify the best time to work with them and optimise their learning. Some children prefer to do homework as soon as they come home from school whilst their concentration is still focussed. For others, the last thing they want to do is more schoolwork when they get home, and need to let off pent up emotion. Some parents have shared with me that their children work well after the evening meal when they are relaxed and ready for bed. On the other hand, some parents say their children are too tired to concentrate at that time. When is your child more receptive to learning?

! Remember: Make time to talk with your children. They come to appreciate their "quality time".

You have your own needs too. Children must learn to understand that you have to manage your time and that you can't always drop every-thing when they want you to. It is important that you explain why you can't help at that moment but that you *will* help them later at a time specified by you and agreed by them. Make sure you then stick to this agreement.

This way, the child learns to trust in what you say and learns that you consider talking and listening to them to be important. Your interest in their schoolwork shows that their attainment is something you value and that you are there to help and support them.

"Learning to Learn' has enabled me to improve my communication skills with effective listening and questioning techniques for me, but especially with my own children."
Gillian McDonald, parent

! Remember: Always respond to children's questions, even if you don't know the answer, or they may learn to stop asking! It is important to be honest. It's all right to say, "I don't know, but we'll find out together!"

What question do you most commonly ask your child when he come home from school? Is it to ask if he's "had a good day?" Answer: no. Another classic is "what did you do at school today?" Answer: nothing. This kind of "closed question" invites the child respond automatically, without giving the question much thought. Try to structure your question more openly. You could, for example, ask, "What's the most interesting thing you did at school today?" thus encouraging thought, analysis and evaluation.

! Remember: Encourage your children to develop their thinking skills by asking "open" questions, which get them to analyse and evaluate a situation.

A third common questioning strategy is "nonproductive" negative questioning. Avoid this approach completely. It can be very intimidating to the child. An example is, "You've been a good girl today, haven't you?" This puts the child in an awkward position. You are directing the child into giving a response that you want to hear rather than inviting her to discuss her day. She may need to talk about something that has happened, and nonproductive questions do not allow her to, because she feels the weight of your expectations!

! Remember: Be honest. If you don't know the answer, say so!

Coping with jargon

Throughout our lives we are constantly faced with jargon. Different professions inevitably develop their own vocabularies and it takes confidence for the nonspecialist to be able to ask the expert, "What do you mean?" Effective communication is a two-way process. There is equal responsibility on speaker and the listener to make themselves clear and to understand what is being said. Have you ever returned from a visit to the doctor unclear about exactly what was said to you? Often we accept the professional judgment of the expert without fully understanding his or her language.

! Remember: Communication is a two-way process. Each party has a responsibility to ensure they are clear in what they are trying to convey.

Teachers have their own language, too, and often slip into "education speak" when talking to parents. Terms such as "baseline assessment", "SATs", "SNUTs" and "national curriculum levels" are the shorthand of their everyday communication and it's easy to forget that many non-teachers don't understand it all. There is no reason why any parent *should* understand these terms without first having them explained, and you will find the meanings of the acronyms above and many other abbreviations and "teacher-speak" in the Glossary on page 127.

To be effective partners in a child's education, we parents need to be able to communicate with the professionals and to know how to help extend our children's learning at home. We need to be able to ask the right questions!

! Remember: School education is a three-way partnership: home–child–school. Each element must contribute to make the partnership truly effective.

Think about the last school parents' evening you attended. Did you passively receive a short report about your child's progress or did you have the opportunity to ask all you wanted to know and discuss future plans and targets?

For many parents, going to the school's open evening triggers negative memories of their own schooldays. It is easy to slip back into a role where you may lack confidence or assertiveness. Parents should be active partners in their children's education. They are the single most important factor in raising the attainment levels of their children. They are the key to creating and nurturing a learning culture at home, an environment where education, in its broadest sense, is valued as important.

In order to work towards a partnership with your child's school, you need to be able to ask the questions that will support and extend your child's learning in the home. The school is required by law to have a 'home-school agreement' (see Glossary on page 127). Have you signed it?

"I would dread my teenagers bringing their homework home as I knew it would end up like World War Three. Now, instead of criticising, I am a lot calmer with them as I have more confidence in myself. I sit down and, if they're having a problem, I say, 'Why don't you do this instead?' "

Janine Bradley, parent of two teenage boys

Questions for the teacher!

Look at the following examples of questions a parent might use when discussing his child's progress at a school open evening:

1. "You say my child is doing well, but what can we do to help him improve further?"
2. "Would you please give me a breakdown of the topics that you're covering in school and some suggestions of how we might extend this learning in the home?"
3. How can I help move my child up to the next level?
4. Can you recommend any resources, or activities we can do together, to help her understand the topic she is about to study?
5. "You say he is having difficulty with maths [for example]. What different teaching strategies have you used that suit his learning style?"

By the end of this book you will, we hope, have a greater understanding of some of the current thinking on learning styles and why *teaching* styles must be varied in order to match the variety of learning styles that exists within a class of pupils.

! Remember: You *can* make a difference!

In summary

- Be aware of how you communicate with your children.
- Listen to them and set aside quality time for talking.
- Try to ask "open" questions to encourage them to think and evaluate their own actions.
- Try to avoid "nonproductive" questions, especially with adolescents
- Ensure language is clear and unambiguous.
- Always answer questions or the child may learn to stop asking!
- Be supportive through success as well as setbacks.

! Remember: Parents need to show children that they are interested, supportive and encouraging in their efforts, being sure to praise them for their successes and helping to overcome setbacks!

Chapter 3

The Right Conditions for Learning

An effective learning environment checklist

One important way you can help support and maximise your child's learning potential is to create the right environment for learning in the home. Here are some ideas.

An appropriate work space

If you are short of space in the home, negotiate with your child where he thinks he would be most comfortable. This may mean using the dining or kitchen table.

Alternatively he may prefer his bedroom. Wherever he chooses, try to ensure that this space is well lit and is clear of clutter, so he has plenty of room to spread out books and equipment. A dedicated space to work in indicates that study is important.

! Remember: Having a work area indicates that study is important.

Minimize distractions

If there are siblings in the house, they should show consideration and be asked to keep noise to a minimum. Try to keep this in mind when planning the dedicated work area. Try to avoid loud music, TV or computer games while children are working.

Certain types of music, such as classical, may help create an atmosphere for learning.

! Remember: Try to avoid too many distractions.

Plan time

You know your child better than anyone else and will know when she's likely to work best. For some it may be when she comes home from school and is still in "work mode". For other children the last thing they want to do is work as soon as they come home. Many just want to let off steam, play, socialise with friends or simply relax in front of the TV.

Some children work best after the evening meal and before bed; others are too tired by then. It is important that you negotiate when is best for your child and for you so that you are available to support her if she needs your help.

Help plan your child's time by identifying what she needs to do during that week. Planning the week's homework, for example, may mean that it is completed well before it has to be handed in – and family stress levels are greatly reduced!

! Remember: You know your child better than anyone else!

Meet basic physical needs

A child will not work well if he's hungry, thirsty, tired, cold or irritated. He will be easily distracted. It is therefore important that these needs be considered.

Research has shown that a good healthy diet with plenty of water helps the brain to function more efficiently. It is also important to work in a well-ventilated room, because this increases the oxygen available to the brain, enabling it to function more effectively. Allow your child plenty of short breaks. Memory is more efficient if learning is broken down into shorter periods of activity rather than one long session.

Drinking water before study can help the brain to perform more efficiently; at the very least, plain water is more healthy than sugar-filled fizzy drinks!

Be there for support!

Be on hand to answer questions, to offer encouragement and to show you are interested in your child's efforts. This raises the status of learning in the home and also helps build healthy relationships with your child.

Be prepared to listen to your child.

! Remember: Be available to offer support and encouragement should your child need it.

In summary

- Ensure your child has a study area away from as many distractions as possible.
- Make sure his/her basic needs are met.
- Negotiate a time when you can make yourself available to offer practical help and support if needed.
- Try to make learning fun and interesting using a variety of resources that will appeal to different learning styles.
- Always remember to praise and encourage children's efforts, however modest.

Chapter 4

Building a Healthier Brain for Learning

Modern science is providing us with exciting information about our brains and how they work when we learn new skills, solve problems and remember things. It is useful to understand on a simple level what some of these findings actually mean in terms of how we can contribute to effective learning.

1. Our brains have a limitless capacity to learn. Technology is teaching us that our brains are even more complicated and sophisticated than we ever could have imagined.

So: Never forget that we are all remarkable and have fantastic potential!

2. 'Thoughts' and ideas are made in the connections between 'neuron' brain cells. We have approaching 100 billion brain cells, each of which is capable of connecting with the others through networks linked together in our brain.

So: We all have the ability to generate an almost infinite number of thoughts, making our capacity to learn enormous.

3. Scientists who did experiments on rats were looking to see what effect stimulation had on the development of intelligence. They found that, when a group of rats were placed in cages with lots of challenging mazes and puzzles to solve, they flourished. But those which were kept in empty cages were aggressive, slovenly and unhealthy. The brain learns new information by making connections. The more connections we can make, the more ideas we can create.

So: Give your children plenty to think about, challenge them and make their lives full of rich experiences. Try to give them opportunities to develop through activities which are fun and challenging.

4. The brain is made up of over 80 per cent liquid. Much of the brain's activity is based on electrical signals. Water in cerebral-spinal fluid enables electricity to be conducted effectively between nerve cells in the brain. Too little water intake can slow the production of cerebral-spinal fluid and reduce the level of nutrients reaching the brain.

So: Ensure your child drinks plenty of plain water. (Most flavoured soft drinks don't count, because the brain and the digestive system do not treat them the same way as clear water – in fact some scientists believe that these so called *diuretics*, including coffee and tea are actually bad for the brain.)

5. Some experts believe that we can actually remember everything we ever see, experience, hear, smell and taste. Knowing *how* to recall the information is the problem!

So: Practise memory strategies (e.g. chunking, association, mnemonics – all explained later) with the confidence that you *do* have the ability to remember a seemingly infinite amount of information.

6. The brain requires oxygen to nourish and energise it. Exercise and a good air supply will increase the flow of oxygen to the brain and allow it to function more effectively.

So: Make sure your child does not become a 'couch potato', but exercises regularly and ensure that there is good ventilation in the room where she studies.

7. Researchers on learning believe that our feelings of well-being are controlled largely by the left prefrontal cortex. Solving problems and having good recall can be affected and limited by the chemicals released by this part of the brain.

> **So:** Never forget that smiles, praise, understanding, love and affection all affect the way the child feels and can help to produce better-motivated and more confident learners.

8. "Daydreaming" is one of the brain's natural ways of exercising creativity and can actually lead to very original and diverse thinking.

> **So:** Encourage your child to imagine "what if?", especially where his optimistic views of the future are concerned. Encourage creative and imaginative play, role-playing, empathy and thinking from others' points of view.

9. Like the muscles of the body, the brain needs to be exercised. Use it, or, like an unhealthy body, it will become flabby and sluggish and its strength will disappear!

> **So:** Develop creative-thinking skills to increase the connections in the brain by trying to link things together. Try to see how one thing is like another. Make it a game to try to connect things. Start with things which have obvious connections: How is Spain like Greece? How is this film like that film? Then play the game of connecting things that don't have obvious connections. How is a dog like a tree? How is an apple like a car? How is …? And so on.
>
> Try some of the exercises in the "Thinking skills" chapters.

10. The area of the brain used for processing emotional responses is also closely connected to the area which is responsible for forming "long-term" memories. Called the 'limbic' area, it acts a bit like a good secretary and decides how important the piece of information is and whether it will be 'significant' in our lives or by helping us to solve a problem or understand something better. A good example of this

might be what has been called the 'cocktail party effect', whereby in a noisy and crowded room with lots of people talking we might suddenly hear our own name being spoken clearly, because it is significant and matters to us.

So: Try to add positive emotions (fun, humour, surprise, novelty etc.) to the learning activity in order to make it more memorable.

11. Our brains continue to solve problems even after we consciously stop thinking about them. People have an instinct to connect things together, complete unfinished problems and to see things through that intrigue them. This is why we often wake up and remember the name of the actor we puzzled over, or where we left our keys or credit card!

So: Don't *rush* to give your child all of the answers. Give her interesting things to think about such as "What if …?", " I wonder what would have happened if …", "Why do you think that?" then return to the unanswered question later.

12. Some brains like to grasp the 'big picture' before looking at details, in order to spot 'patterns' and understand connections.

For example, look at this illustration – which letter do you see first?

More than likely it would have been the "H", and then you would see it is made up of s's.

Health check for your brain

Drink plenty of water

Fill the brain with oxygen through regular exercise

Cut out sugary drinks, coffee and tea

Give the brain time to process the day's information – get plenty of sleep!

Plan time for relaxation

Feed the brain with lots of different sorts of information and stimulation (not just computer games)

Make learning fun, varied, active

Building a healthy brain – checklist

- Drink plenty of water
- Cut out sugary drinks, coffee and tea
- Feed the brain with lots of different sorts of information and stimulation (not just computer games)
- Fill the brain with oxygen through regular exercise
- Give the brain time to process the day's information – get plenty of sleep!
- Make learning fun, varied, active
- Plan time for relaxation.

Part 2

Learning About Learning – Practical Strategies for Parents to Use

Chapter 5

Mind Mapping®

Mind Mapping®[2] is a technique which was developed by Tony Buzan, who is an authority on the brain, memory and creativity. He invented the skill of Mind Mapping® in response to his own difficulties in learning effectively while at university. It is a technique that appeals to children and adults regardless of their preferred learning style.

Mind Mapping® has a variety of uses, two of the major ones being creative thinking and memorising.

Mind Mapping® can be a fast and spontaneous method of planning on paper. Buzan estimates that there is a saving of 90 per cent of the time that it would take to make traditional notes. It is effective because of the way it works with the brain's natural habit of associating and connecting information.

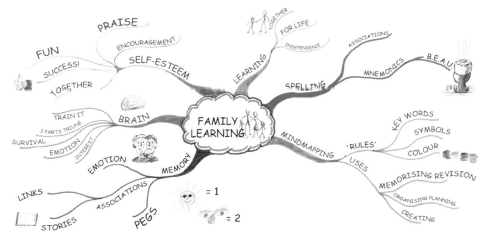

Each of our billion-plus brain cells is programmed to grow 'branches' called axons which act as tracks for thoughts and ideas. It is therefore a very natural pattern of the thinking process to connect things together in a 'radiant' way, as new ideas occur and link to the topic or theme.

---

[2] Mind Maps® is a registered trademark of The Buzan Organisation.

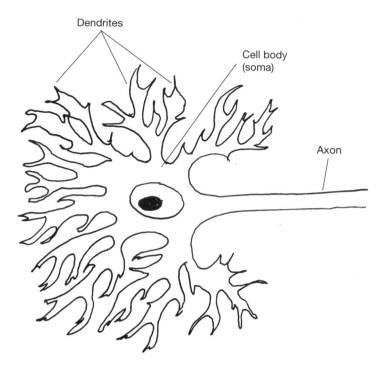

Dendrites

Cell body
(soma)

Axon

The structure of the Mind Map® resembles the way in which the brain makes associations and links between ideas. Not only does the speed of mind mapping avoid inhibiting creativity, but the process itself seems to assist with the generation of new ideas.

Mind Maps® also have the advantage of being easily added to with each branch representing a paragraph or section of the final piece of work.

Mind Mapping® is a bit like putting your signature on something. It does not matter that your Mind Maps® are incomprehensible to others, as long as the images and symbols you use are significant enough to be memorable to you. The very process of inventing codes and symbols helps the brain to store information and puts its connecting powers to good effect.

Repetition is vital to learning. A Mind Map®, even one that includes a large amount of material, may be reviewed in just a few minutes, allowing you to go through the entire material daily, reading key words only.

Getting started with Mind Mapping®

The basic technique of Mind Mapping® is very quick to learn but, like anything, practice makes perfect.

Some children may feel uncomfortable with some of the conventions, such as writing in capital letters, using only key words, including pictures and symbols and using colour. It is important to emphasise that a Mind Map® is something personal to them and that, although they may wish to show it to other people, it is what their Mind Map® means to them that is most important.

This may be particularly true for children who feel they are not as good at drawing as others and who may resist the emphasis on creativity. Stress that the symbols and pictures are to help them, and that it does not matter if others do not recognise what they were intended to be!

How to make a Mind Map®

You will need a variety of coloured felt-tip pens and a large sheet of paper.

Step 1
Turn the paper to landscape orientation and write your main idea in the middle. Use at least three colours for this section of your mind map and include a picture or symbol of what the central idea is.

Step 2
Then for each main idea, draw large, bold branches leading off from the central idea. The branches should be the same length as wording of the main ideas, and each should be a different colour.

Step 3
Draw smaller branches leading off from the key words for each sub-idea. These are connected, but less important ideas. Use symbols, pictures, codes and shorthand in your Mind Maps®. These will help you to remember what you are learning.

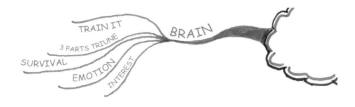

The uses of Mind Maps®

You can use Mind Maps® for lots of different purposes in school and at home.

Lots of people use Mind Maps® to help them to learn work by heart, especially when they are getting ready for tests.

Actually drawing the Mind Map® itself is a useful way of beginning to memorise your work, especially if you include lots of colour and symbols. You can then look over the Mind Map® frequently with your child (each evening before sleep is a good idea).

The more times you look at something, the more likely you are to remember it (especially if you have to 'do something' such as interpret the meaning). A Mind Map®, even if it covers many pages of notes from an exercise book, can be reviewed in minutes and also be an exercise in thinking and interpretation.

It is very easy to learn how to Mind Map®. You might like to try to make a Mind Map® on any of the following topics.

- A topic covered at school (or work)
- Ideas for a story
- Planning a family holiday

Clockwise©

Clockwise© is a simple variation of the Mind Map® formula of writing things down using visual images and symbols. The difference is that in this case your child should write or draw the images in a 'chronological' order around the central clock structure, i.e. *as* they occurred.

If for example you wanted to remember **the order of the Tudor kings and queens** and some of the key details of their reigns:

- At 12 o'clock you could draw symbols to represent Henry VII, the Wars of the Roses, his marriage, etc;
- Perhaps at 2 o'clock you would draw Henry VIII, symbols and pictures to represent the key events in his reign;
- At 6 o'clock you might draw Edward and pictures to represent his short reign;
- At 7 o'clock Mary and her activities;
- At 8 o'clock Queen Elizabeth and the great achievements of her age.

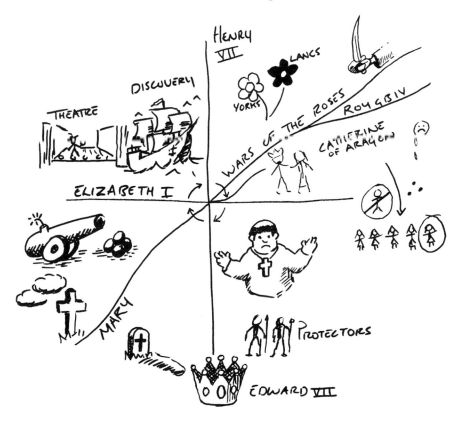

Clockwise© is a fun way of writing down in a visual way important information which has to be learned or organised.

Think about how you might use this to help plan a story, a family event, or to remember important details in order.

Chapter 6

Learning Styles

"Preferred" learning styles

We are constantly receiving information about the world around us from our senses. The most obvious of these in school learning is through our eyes, ears and bodies. These ways of receiving information about the world around us can influence the preferred style of learning we develop.

In *Head Start: How to Develop Your Child's Mind* (1999), Robert Fisher writes:

In a typical class of thirty children more than twenty will be able to take in information in three different ways – visually (through seeing), auditorily (through hearing), and kinaesthetically (through touching). Two or three children will have problems learning in any of these ways. The rest, about six of them, will have a strongly favoured style, either visual, auditory or kinaesthetic.

People organise and connect new information in their brains in different ways. If we learn something well in a particular way, the chances are we will also remember the feeling of pleasure we experienced from achieving this. If, for example, we enjoy learning well by doing something physical or by movement, this might become our preferred learning style. Thus the association of pleasure with the way of doing something can become a strong one and cause us to tend towards doing things that way again in the future. Sometimes a teacher may teach something in a way that doesn't necessarily suit your child's preferred style of learning. Being resourceful and adaptable means finding a way to overcome this problem.

- People who have a preference for *visual* styles of learning will like to see things and to visualise them.

49

- People who prefer an *auditory* mode prefer to listen and talk through new ideas.
- People who prefer a *kinaesthetic* mode of learning like to touch, feel or do something in a practical way.

Which is the best learning style?

The answer is that there is no one style of learning that is "better" than another, although sometimes working with an inappropriate style can make learning difficult.

For example if you were going to learn spelling skills, using 'visual' ways of learning might help you remember more effectively how the word looked. If you were trying to remember a new spelling using 'auditory' learning strategies, you might find the whole process very difficult.

Try learning words such as "psychology" using sound patterns only and you could easily end up with "sykolodjy".

 It is better to know that you should be adaptable and ready to change the learning style you are using in order to fit the task.

Learners who stick only to a 'preferred style' often lose out. Smart learners use *all styles* in different situations. For example, some learners find revising their own notes before tests by simply reading them over again extremely boring and not very effective. By reading the notes aloud or turning them into a radio play and recording them on to tape, the learning can become much more memorable and fun!

Assess your learning style

If you were to learn something new, which would you prefer to do? Tick the description that best suits your preferred learning style.

Visual
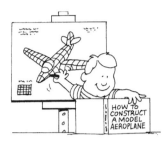
- ❏ make pictures, Mind Maps®, doodles
- ❏ watch videos or television
- ❏ watch a demonstration
- ❏ read a book
- ❏ imagine I'm doing something
- ❏ see a map or picture

Auditory

- ❏ listen to information that has been put to music
- ❏ listen to some explanation
- ❏ have discussions and hear different people's ideas
- ❏ listen to the radio, tapes or CDs
- ❏ talk to myself about what I am doing or learning
- ❏ when I read to myself I like to hear a voice reading to me

Kinaesthetic

- ❏ move around a lot to learn
- ❏ learn through games, sport, dance, drama
- ❏ learn through copying others
- ❏ do something as I am learning, e.g. writing, underlining, doodling
- ❏ learn through practice
- ❏ learn through experiments, e.g. on computers, in cooking, making something
- ❏ learn by making things, e.g. models, games

Do you find you have a *preferred* way of learning or do you use a range of strategies? Try to assess your own child to see if you are similar. If not, then possibly this may explain other differences between you, such as your hobbies or interests.

How can I help my child?

A good, versatile learner will be able to use as many different approaches as possible to learn the required information and even a combination of approaches in order to make more connections in his or her brain. Don't get stuck in just one style of learning, try a variety of approaches.

Visual learning
- make posters and maps
- watch videos
- read books
- collect photographs
- use highlighter pens to colour-code information
- identify CD-ROMs, websites
- see plays and musicals
- draw Mind Maps®

Auditory learning
- discuss ideas together
- read aloud
- use tapes to record ideas and to play back frequently
- choose suitable background music
- put things to music
- practise chanting and singing the information

Kinaesthetic (hands-on) learning
- visit places such as historical sites, museums
- act out sequences and events
- make models and props
- give demonstrations, re-enactments
- visit places associated with the topic being studied
- use cameras, video cameras, tape recorders.

Chapter 7

Multiple Intelligences

Understanding intelligence

As every parent knows, each of their children is uniquely different and possesses interests and talents that may not necessarily be shared by brothers and sisters, even in the case of twins! Parents sometimes suffer terrible anxiety about whether or not their children are "keeping up" with their friends or peers. And how many of us have ever said or thought, "He's got better concentration than his elder brother" or "She's not as shy as her elder sister"?

Sometimes comparisons such as these can lead us to judge children unfairly because they assume that all children's abilities can be measured in the same way. Our expectations of a younger brother or sister can often lead us to underestimate or even neglect the true abilities he or she possesses. Ideally, we should avoid making comparisons between children, because they can generate damaging feelings of inferiority and resentment.

 Comparing one child's *intelligence* with another's can be especially damaging.

You may already have some ideas about what being "intelligent" means and what types of people fit into that picture. It is very likely that people like Leonardo da Vinci, Albert Einstein, William Shakespeare and Winston Churchill might be among those you considered. It is probably less likely that famous musicians such as Eric Clapton, artists such as David Hockney, sportspeople such as David Beckham or performers such as Billy Connolly and Anthony Hopkins would be listed, even though they also demonstrate an enormous amount of intelligence to excel at what they do.

At one parents' evening, a mother sat down with her daughter and said, within her poor girl's hearing, that her child was "only average". Unfortunately, in this particular parent's eyes, this is all her little girl would ever be. All children are special and unique and possess enormous potential. So upon what did she base this observation? And why should we believe she was wrong?

The theory that we all possess a wide *range* of talents through which we can demonstrate intelligence was first put forward by the American psychologist Howard Gardner in his book 'Frames of Mind' (1983). He argues that intelligence is shown when we "make things or solve problems which are useful to the society we live in", and that this can take many different forms. For example, a problem that needs to be solved by a London stockbroker might not be the same as a problem that needs to be solved by a person born and brought up in the Amazon rainforest. Both might be of equal value to the society they live in.

This is now accepted by many people in education as among the most important thinking to have emerged in recent years about the way we learn.

What are the "multiple intelligences"?

Gardner has recently claimed that we might possess nine or more intelligences which we might use to solve problems and make things of value to our society. It is important to understand this if we are to appreciate the many different ways our own children can show "intelligence".

Here is a very brief summary of our intelligences:

Intelligence type	Aptitude or preference for:
Linguistic	Word related activities, such as writing
Logical	Solving problems involving logic, numbers
Visual	Visual information, images, pictures
Musical	Sound-related activities
Bodily	Activities involving movement or making things
Interpersonal	Good people skills, communication, management
Philosophical (intrapersonal)	Independence, thoughtfulness, self-awareness
Natural	Anything related to nature, the seasons, the universe
Spiritual	Religious, cosmic and mystical awareness

So, instead of worrying whether or not your child *is* intelligent, start thinking *how* he is intelligent.

"The importance of Howard Gardner's theory is this. We've moved from 'How smart are you?' to 'How are you smart?'"

Colin Rose, 1999

Test yourself

Below is a simple test that should give an insight of which intelligences you feel you have developed strengths in and which still require some work. Tick the statements that you feel apply most to you.

Linguistic
- ❑ I like plays, poetry, books, radio, conversation
- ❑ I learn well from books, tapes and listening to others
- ❑ I am a good and interesting speaker
- ❑ I can explain things well
- ❑ I like to write things down
- ❑ I am good at remembering conversations and quotes

Total:

Logical
- ❑ I like to solve puzzles and problems
- ❑ I like clear step-by-step explanations
- ❑ I arrange things in a sensible and well-ordered way
- ❑ I often look for patterns and links between things
- ❑ If I have a problem I solve it in a step-by-step way
- ❑ I enjoy detective stories and films

Total:

Visual
- ❑ I have a good sense of direction
- ❑ I often see things other people don't notice
- ❑ I can remember visual details well

❑   It helps me to learn when I can see films, slides and videos
❑   I can easily use diagrams, maps, charts and graphs
❑   I like to get the big picture of what's going on

Total:

Physical
❑   I enjoy activities such as sports and dancing
❑   I enjoy DIY and car maintenance
❑   I like rough-and-tumble games
❑   My hobbies include sport, walking, activity
❑   I like cooking, baking, cake decorating
❑   I like painting, decorating and handicrafts

Total:

Musical
❑   I am interested in music
❑   I like playing music
❑   I have a good sense of timing
❑   I have a good sense of rhythm
❑   I can easily remember lyrics to songs
❑   I don't like silence

Total:

Personal
❑   I enjoy working in groups
❑   I like taking part in clubs
❑   I am interested in how others feel and think
❑   I notice other people's mood changes and reactions
❑   I am a good mediator
❑   I enjoy being in the company of lots of people

Total:

Philosophical
❑   I like to daydream and imagine things
❑   I prefer my own company

❏   I like to work in quieter places
❏   I try to understand why I feel as I do about things
❏   I think about the reasons for doing things
❏   I ask myself questions about my reasons for doing things

Total:

Natural
❏   I enjoy being outdoors
❏   I like animals and birds
❏   I like flowers and most living, growing things
❏   I am conscious of the weather and seasons
❏   I am interested in environmental issues
❏   I am interested in the working functions of living things

Total:

Spiritual
❏   I think about life-and-death issues
❏   I enjoy finding out about religions
❏   I like stories with a spiritual theme
❏   I like thinking about deep questions
❏   I enjoy choir and church music written to evoke spiritual feelings
❏   I find questions about religion and the universe fascinating

Total:

Look at the intelligences you have ticked more frequently. This should provide a basic insight into your intelligence profile – which intelligences are already well developed, and which you should concentrate on strengthening.

Using your intelligences to learn

These ideas may be useful in helping your child to revise a topic or to learn something new. Instead of just trying to learn something in one way, experiment with other ways of exploring the topic and bring into play your multiple intelligences! Don't be afraid to mix up the different approaches or even to add new ones to make the learning more adventurous and fun.

Linguistic
- Summarise the information into your own words.
- Make keyword posters.
- Make up a list of self-test questions that can be answered with "yes" or "no".
- Devise puzzles and board games based on the topic.

Logical
- Sort things into categories and lists.
- Look for patterns, sequences, order.
- Create flowcharts with step-by-step accounts of the topic.

Visual
- Make a Mind Map®.
- Draw a cartoon/poster of the information.
- Watch videos/live demonstrations of the material.

Musical
- Choose appropriate background music for inspiration and atmosphere.
- Try to put information into poem, song or rap form.
- Choose music that goes with the topic, e.g. World War One and *The Planets*.

Personal
- Share ideas with someone else, have a "study buddy".
- Teach others, or lead a revision lesson.
- Make lists of questions to interview each other about the topic.

Philosophical
- Keep a diary or learning log.
- Link your ideas to personal or family experiences.
- Write down important questions that occur to you about the topic.

Physical
- Pay a visit to a museum, site or place connected to the topic.
- Use Post-it[3] notes to write down information (play games by moving them around etc. – guess which one is missing).
- Make up games, charades and so on that involve movement.

Natural
- When visiting an area connected with your topic find out about the local geography, wildlife and marine life.
- Be aware of the role of the natural world in your topic (climate, weather, animals, food production, for instance).
- Make collections of natural artefacts connected with your topic.

Spiritual
- Watch films connected with your study area that have big moral and spiritual themes, such as *Schindler's List*, or *The Green Mile.*
- Visit churches, temples, mosques and other places of religious significance.
- Collect prints or postcards of works of art connected with your topic that deal with spiritual themes or seem to address aspects of spiritual life.

In conclusion Multiple Intelligence theory shows us that...

- There are a variety of ways that children can show intelligence other than in different types of intelligence tests.
- Intelligence is not based on a fixed number that cannot be improved. We can all develop our less-used intelligences.
- There is more than one way of learning something (we can tap into all of our intelligences to learn something new).
- Learning can be so much more fun when we try different ways of doing things.
- Parents can understand the reasons why their children might have different strengths and weaknesses and be able to help them more effectively.

---

[3] The Post-it® brand is a registered trademark of 3M

Chapter 8

Solving Problems

Improving your child's thinking skills for learning

There is a vast range of thinking skills that your child will develop to become a more effective learner. In this chapter we will share ideas for activities which can help you to practice some of these skills with your child. Hopefully this will help you feel more confident to experiment with your own ways to improve different aspects of your child's creative thinking.

What is 'problem-solving'?

At work, at home and at school, we are constantly being challenged with problems that need to be solved. Some people rise to the challenges and see them as opportunities: they have clear and effective systems for tackling problems, which in turn gives them a greater sense of self-confidence. Other people fear the challenge of solving problems. They have few skills (or none at all) to call on when tackling problems. Often this is because no matter how minor or trivial the problem may be; they fail to identify the nature of the problem – that means that they are not able to recognise what skills they already have that would help to solve the problem, so they are not in a good position to apply the correct tools to solve it. This need not always be the case.

Parents can help children to think of problems as challenges that can *always* be overcome. If we can first help children to work out *how* problems may be broken down into manageable parts, we can begin to develop crucial thinking strategies for problem solving. This approach will provide children with many valuable skills that they can apply time and time again in many learning situations.

For example, my five-year old daughter is a jigsaw puzzle *expert*. She is never intimidated by even the largest of puzzles because she has developed an effective and systematic problem-solving strategy for jig-saws. She breaks the exercise down into smaller parts! First of all, she collects together the straight-edged pieces; then she looks for strong colours that connect together, then faces, clothes or buildings, while all the time studying the big picture on the box to give her guidance.

What's the problem? Analysis and synthesis

Problem solving can be more effective when the task is broken down into smaller, separate but related parts. The process of breaking a problem down into simpler pieces has itself two parts. Scientists call these two processes 'analysis' and 'synthesis'.

Analysis is the ability to break a problem down into sub-parts in order to see how they fit together.

Synthesis is the ability to put the parts of the problem back together in a way that solves the problem. This is precisely what Grace's jigsaw-solving strategy includes.

One famous problem solving activity is called the Tower of Hanoi, invented by Edouard Lucas in 1883. A number of discs are placed on a peg at one end of a three-peg board with the smallest at the top:

The object of the exercise is to get all the discs from the left hand peg to the right hand peg, with the largest disc at the bottom again. The only problem is that you may not place a larger disc on top of a smaller one. A quick look on the internet will offer many ways to solve the puzzle but the point is that once you can understand how the puzzle works (the *knack* of it) it's easy to solve. However, it is often this initial stage of problem solving, understanding the core of the problem that causes children (and adults) the greatest difficulty.

Improving analysis

What steps can we take as parents to help children to grasp the point that problems *can* be broken down into more manageable parts? Start by showing your child how problems can be solved by breaking them down. The following ideas might help you.

Self-assembly syndrome

If you have ever tried your hand at DIY, you have no doubt come across the self-assembly syndrome more times than you care to recall. Ever found extra pieces in the box *after* you have finished putting the item together?

If you feel brave enough, you might be prepared to allow your children to experiment with taking apart a self-assembly object such as a coffee table or some shelves and let them figure out how to put them back together again. Maybe you could start with a toy or some Lego bricks. From simple exercises like these, children can begin to grasp that there are potential problem-solving activities all around them.

"What is it made up of?"

Start by looking at the picture of the £5 note in the illustration overleaf. Ask your child how it is connected to the six coins. The answer might be rather obvious to adults but may need explaining to younger children. Be prepared to ask your child if there are any other coins that could be used in different combinations to make the same total. In the case of the cherry bun, he might be encouraged to add missing ingredients. In the case of the aeroplane it might be that he adds the extra ingredients needed to make the model.

Detectives

Take a selection of household objects (some ideas are listed below). You can put them all in one bag or lay them on a table. Tell your child that he's a detective and that you are going to build up a picture of a mystery person. He has to use all of the clues to make a composite picture of who the owner might be.

Encourage your child to think about each clue carefully before jumping to a conclusion.

- a penknife
- two 20 pence pieces
- a passport photograph with the name David Edwards on the back
- a necklace
- some chewing gum
- a woman's compact

All of these activities and tasks will encourage children to appreciate that problems are always made up of smaller parts. As they begin to become aware that problems can be broken down into pieces try to encourage your child to use the same strategies to tackle school and homework problems (and not just maths!)

Here is a game you might like to try playing in the car, on a train or during a long bus journey.

Make up a story that includes all of the following (give a time limit of one minute to make up and tell the story):

- a broken umbrella
- a dog
- a sweet wrapper

Or ...

* a broken key
* a dead bird
* a flooded lane

... and so on.

When each player has finished, they can make up three new ingredients for the next.

Writing frames

Sometimes, just the thought of a long piece of writing can be quite intimidating for a child. This feeling can be calmed if the task is broken up into smaller, more manageable parts and given a structure through a "writing frame". Learning to use writing frames can help your child to write more effectively by *breaking down* the whole task into smaller parts.

When your child gets "stuck" and doesn't know *what* to write or even *how* to begin, you can provide her with a simple writing frame, listing the key points to include and some ideas on how to start off and finish. Often, giving your child the first line of a story will be enough to set off a burst of creative activity.

Many schools and businesses have standard letters that they send to people, adjusting the personal details to match the recipient. These standard letters are writing frames. The frame provides a structure for the person writing the letter to focus on the important information he or she needs to include. For example, this standard letter for informing a parent of a success at school (see Letter 'A' opposite).

The teacher simply fills in the blanks to complete the letter, which is typed up in one consistent font (see Letter 'B' opposite).

Using this writing frame ensures that everybody includes the appropriate information and everybody follows the same standard format. In other words, the task has been broken down into smaller steps through the different prompts on the frame.

Dear _____

I am delighted to inform you that your son/daughter _____
has achieved ___ positive merits from _____ to _____ and has
therefore been awarded a _____ college certificate.

As you are aware, _____ awards are not gained easily and
this is a testimony to _____'s hard work and commitment this
term.

Yours sincerely

M. Gorman
(Headteacher)

Letter A

Dear **Mrs Tug**

I am delighted to inform you that your son **Brent** has achieved **50** positive merits from **September** to **December 2003** and has therefore been awarded a **silver** college certificate.

As you are aware, **silver** awards are not gained easily and this is a testimony to **Brent**'s hard work and commitment this term.

Yours sincerely

M. Gorman
(Headteacher)

Letter B

You can use a writing frame to help your child with other kinds of writing, particularly non-fiction writing. With more practice he can create his own writing frames, beginning to draft letters and stories before filling in the details – this is the way most professionals write.

Kinds of writing

There are, of course, many different kinds of writing, for different purposes and for different audiences. An eyewitness account will be very different from an argumentative or discussion-type essay. It is possible to create a writing frame for each of them:

1. **Report**: This is usually written to describe how something is: e.g. a report of an experiment or investigation. Broken down into smaller components, a typical frame might look like the following:

    I decided to find out about _____

    because _____.

    I already knew that _____.

    The aspects I wanted to find more about were _____.

    I discovered that _____.

    The most interesting thing I found out was _____.

    I got this information from _____.

    Your child might be expected to write a report of an experiment in science, research in technology or history.

2. **Procedure**: To explain how something happens in a series of step-by-step operations (such as the water cycle in geography or a description of an activity or piece of theory in physical education), the following frame might be useful:

    The purpose of this essay is to explain how _____.

    The first step is _____.

    It then follows that _____.

    The next step is (etc.) _____.

    Finally, _____

3. **Discussion**: This is an essay-type piece of writing designed to give different points of view and explore different sides of an argument. This might be used in English, citizenship or history.

    There is a lot of discussion about whether _____.

    The people who agree with this idea (such as) _____

    claim that _____.

    They also argue that _____.

    A further point they make is _____.

    However, there are also strong arguments to support the view

    that _____.

    Another argument is _____.

    Furthermore, _____.

    After looking at the different points of view and the evidence for

    them, I think _____,

    because _____.

Try composing writing frames for the following examples that will help to support your child with writing for different purposes.

4. **Recount**: Tell the story of an incident. It will usually be written in the past tense.

5. **Explanation**: Show how something works or why something has happened.

6. **Persuasive**: Promote a particular point of view, or to sell an idea or product.

Synthesis – putting together things we know

Analysis is about breaking a problem into manageable pieces, encouraging your child to examine problems more carefully and think about each of the elements that made them up. The next step is to encourage children to put the parts together so that the problem becomes easy to solve.

In this example the problem involved assembling shaded cubes from their nets (see page 71). In this context, the net is the flat piece of paper, which can be folded into a three dimensional object.

The activity assumes that your child is already clear about the relationship between a net and a 3-D shape. If you are unsure about this, give her some plain paper, a pencil and a ruler and ask her to construct a cube. Remember that the cube should be constructed from one single piece of paper; there should be no need to stick on any extra pieces.

> Now try the activity on page 71. Ask your child to study the page of information and identify which three-dimensional shape comes from each of the three nets. In each case there is only one correct answer. She should be able to explain to you how she reached her solution. You could make up some or all of the shapes from the nets. These can be used to help children explain their answers or for you to explain the right answers.

Where else can we use this skill?
It can be useful to think of other items around the house that work on the same principle and allow your child the opportunity to explore these activities (for example, containers for gifts or cakes, flat-packed containers for food and so on).

This kind of thinking can help with:

*   writing essays (e.g. breaking down the problem into smaller parts before constructing an answer – see the section above on writing frames)
*   assignments (forming categories or subtopics to help with developing an answer)
*   design tasks

Sequencing – solving problems by putting things in order

A step-by-step approach is often useful approach to solving problems. It also helps children to understand how to 'sequence' ideas and how different things can be connected together. Again, the examples in this section will be familiar to your child from school and from around the home.

Organising things to make sense – tasks

The following tasks are all similar. They depict everyday activities in which the tasks have to be carefully sequenced in order to avoid mistakes and time wasting. It is a good idea to explain to your child that you are both going to play a game that can be fun but also has a purpose.

Ask him to write down (or tell) as accurately as he can all of the steps necessary to make a cup of tea. Now follow these instructions as literally as you can. Try not to carry out any of the steps that are missing, no matter how obvious!

How effectively have you been able to make a cup of tea?

Talk about what happened with your child; discuss some of the problems which have arisen. Here's a set of instructions to help a novice to make a cup of tea.

Step 1: Fill kettle three-quarters full of cold water from the cold-water tap.
Step 2: Turn on the electric kettle and leave to boil.
Step 3: Put three spoonfuls of tealeaves into the teapot.
Step 4: Pour boiling water from the kettle into the teapot.

While you are discussing this little experiment with your child try to draw out of him which steps had to be done and which steps could have been done in a variety of orders.

Now try the same sequencing tasks using the example sheet on page 73 (you may photocopy this page if you wish). This exercise is designed to show that in some cases a problem needs to be solved in a particular order but in other cases the sequence of steps is not so important.

Sorting into an order can help us to think and learn

Sticky note-lets can be a terrific thinking and learning tool. By placing different pieces of information onto sticky notes, it is possible to play around with the order of information. To complete this activity successfully, your child will examine the cause-and-effect relationships between the pieces of information and should be able to give good explanations for the choices he makes. Encourage your child to explain *why* he believes something to be in the order it is, in every case.

Copy the following lines onto Post-its®, mix them up and, with your child, encourage him to try to put the lines into a "sensible" order (note that there may be several different "sensible" orders, all of which may be thought through, explained and discussed).

Example 1: "Geography" – an explanation of the water cycle

The sun warms oceans, lakes and seas, turning water into vapour, a gas. This is called evaporation.	Plants and trees also breathe out water vapour through tiny holes in their leaves. This is called transpiration.	The air rises. High up, where it's cooler, the water vapour condenses into tiny water droplets. These form clouds.	The clouds are carried along by the wind. The water droplets inside them grow into larger drops, leading to …

The water drops fall as rain (or hail, or sleet, or snow).	Some water runs along the ground and some soaks into it, heading for streams and rivers.	The river carries the water back to the ocean. The cycle is complete.

Example 2: English – Act One, Scene One, of Shakespeare's Macbeth

Thunder and lightning. Enter three witches.	When shall we three meet again in thunder, lightning or in rain?	When the hurlyburly's done, When the battle's lost and won.	That will be ere the set of sun.
Where the place?	Upon the heath.	There to meet with Macbeth.	I come, Graymalkin!
Paddock calls.	Fair is foul and foul is fair …	Hover through the fog and filthy air.	They vanish into mist.

Example 3: Languages – a conversation to book a table at a French restaurant

Bonjour, je voudrais reserver une table, s'il vous plait.	Oui, c'est pour combien de personnes?	Cinq personnes.	Pour quand, monsieur?
Hello, I'd like to reserve a table, please.	Yes, for how many people?	Five people.	For when, sir?

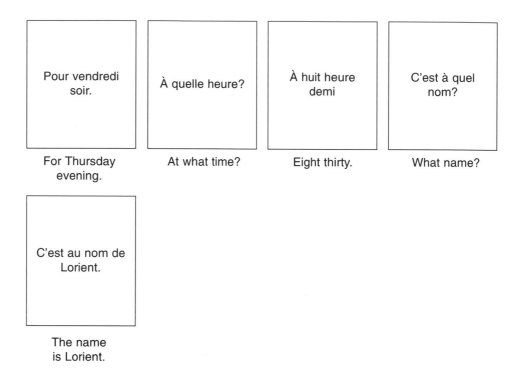

It's important that you talk together with your child about the position and order of the different squares. Move the Post-its® around and experiment with different orders. Try to link them logically with well-reasoned thinking. Consider how this might help learning in lots of other subjects such as science or PE. See how learning something can become "fun" and challenging as you complete the activity together.

Coming up with new ideas – hypothesising

Hypothesising means creating ideas or theories. People who are good at hypothesising often generate many original ideas to find solutions to problems. In this section we hope to highlight some ways to develop some hypothesising skills. Mainly, this means asking lots of different kinds of questions.

Join the dots

Share this problem with your child.

○   ○   ○   ○   ○   ○   ○   ○   ○

○   ○   ○   ○   ○   ○   ○   ○   ○

○   ○   ○   ○   ○   ○   ○   ○   ○

How can you join the nine dots with only four straight lines, without taking your pen or pencil off the paper and without going over the same line twice?

It can be done!

It is tempting to give up in the first stages and to think that this is an impossible task, but, once the solution is known, we wonder how we never thought of it in the first place! (See the solution on page 131.) Once you know the four-line solution, try to think of a way of completing it using only three lines and then by using only one (it can be done).

There is also a message contained in this activity about 'believing that a seemingly impossible task *can* be done'. Remember to reinforce the idea that all problems have solutions which can be discovered through creative and imaginative thinking. This is a very important message to convey to your child.

One thing which should be emphasised to your child is that often it is the 'thinking and questioning *process*, which leads to solving problems. We hope that completing this unit together will encourage your child to ask increasingly creative and probing questions with confidence.

The *right* answer may not always be obvious or easy to find, but the questioning process will open up new channels of creative thinking, which will assist with problem solving and analysis in all sorts of areas of school experience.

Problem solving and "effective questioning"

Becoming reflective (metacognition)
Flexible and resourceful thinkers often think about the processes they used and the kinds of question they used to find a solution to a problem.

When trying to solve a problem, encourage your child to use the following questions:

Q. What am I assuming?
Q. Why am I assuming this?
Q. Which information is irrelevant?
Q. How many possible solutions can I think of?
Q. Do my guesses fit the facts I have?
Q. Is there any other information that I need to know?

And so on.

As we have already discussed, it's important to think about the nature of the problem by breaking it down into more manageable parts; look at details to see what their relevance might be.

Open and closed questions
As we saw in Chapter 2, *closed* questions can only result in a limited answer ('yes' or 'no' usually!). They are questions that may or may not give the kind of information needed. On the other hand, there may be times when you might want a straight 'yes-or-no' answer!

Twenty questions

- Make up twenty questions about your child's favourite TV show or celebrity that could be answered with the word "yes".
- Make up twenty questions about your child's favourite TV show or celebrity that could be answered with the word "no".
- Make a list of single words for your child, who then has to make up "crossword clues" for them.
- Play the *yes and no* game where you ask questions in order to trick each other into saying "yes". The person has to avoid saying it at all costs! For example:

Q. Is your name John?
A. It is.
Q. How old are you?
A. Fifteen.
Q. Fifteen?
A. That's right.

Formulating questions
Encourage your child to experiment with "what if?" questions in order to practice hypothesising.

Remember Kipling's six honest serving men, who taught him all he knew. Their names, he tells us in "The Elephant's Child" (*Just So Stories*, 1902), are What and Why and When and How and Where and Who.

Try to apply some of your child's creative thinking to the following problem. "What if …?" is a crucial key to unlocking the answer.

Antony and Cleopatra

Antony and Cleopatra are lying dead on the floor of an Egyptian villa. Nearby is a broken bowl. There are no marks on their bodies and they were not poisoned. Not a person was in the villa when they died. How did they die?

After one or two minutes, give this clue: "Their deaths followed the accidental breaking of the bowl." (Answer on page 132.)

Prioritising – choosing the relevant information

When you are solving problems, it is important to start thinking carefully about which information is relevant and which is irrelevant.

Choosing relevant information for your answer

The hotel detective

A detective was walking along the corridor of a large hotel one day. Suddenly he heard a woman's voice cry out, "For God's sake don't shoot me, John!" Then there came a shot. He ran to the room from where the shot had come and burst in. In one corner of the room lay a woman who had been shot through the heart. In the middle of the floor was the gun that was used to shoot her. On the other side of the room stood a postman, a lawyer and an accountant. The detective looked at them for a moment and then went up to the postman and said, "I am arresting you for the murder of that woman."

He had never seen any of the people in that room before and yet he was correct in apprehending the postman as the murderer. How did he know?

Give a clue after one or two minutes of the start of deliberations: "No one had any means of identification on them, such as a name badge." (The answer is on page 132.)

When you know the answer, talk to your child about the things you took for granted about the situation and the effectiveness and relevance of the different types of questions you posed.

(The above examples are adapted from Paul Sloane, 1999.)

Here's another sort of information sorting task:

Look at these three questions. Talk about each one with your child. Decide between you which information is relevant and which is irrelevant. Place an "r" next to the piece of information you consider to be relevant, and an "i" next to that you consider irrelevant.

1. **How do light switches work?**
    * The average home has twenty sources of electric light.
    * The electrical current heats a filament in the bulb and this glows to give the light.

- Switches break or complete the circuit required to supply electricity to the bulb.
- Most homes are now lit by electricity.

2. **Why is English the first language of the United States?**
   - English is the most widely spoken language in the world.
   - The US was a British colony before the American War of Independence.
   - English is a peculiar mixture of many different languages, both ancient and modern.
   - English is commonly recognised as the language of air travel.

3. **What makes a steam locomotive move?**
   - A vast complex system of pipes carries steam from the boiler to each of the pistons.
   - Wood or coal is burned in a small furnace in order to heat the water to boiling point.
   - Pistons are forced in and out by the pressure of the steam.
   - The movement of the pistons pushes the wheels around.

(Answers are on page 132.)

(Adapted from *Increase Your Learning Power* (1994).)

Sifting through text for relevant information

Read the following short extracts to your child, and ask the question. Then look at the information again and identify the information which is relevant and irrelevant in each. After each question talk about the *assumptions* made and how you could have explored the problem from a different angle or a different perspective.

1. John and Mary are an odd couple. John drinks only coffee; Mary prefers tea. John eats fatty meat; Mary prefers lean. John hates egg whites; Mary eats only yolks. They are staying in a hotel where, one morning, each orders a full English breakfast to suit his or her tastes.

Question: How many egg whites will be left when the waiter clears the plates?

2.   A peacock roams the grounds of Sir Randolph Jolly's estate. There is a six-metre gap in the twelve-foot-high wall and the peacock strays onto his neighbour's land. "By rights I should keep the eggs laid here, sir," said his neighbour, "but I want the gap repaired, so for each egg I return, I want you to build three square feet of wall."

Question: In order for the gap to be filled, how many eggs did the bird lay?

3.   A huge tanker breaks up in a hurricane, having lurched into a secluded bay for shelter. Despite the frantic efforts of its crew and the coastguard, it leaks thousands of gallons of crude oil. The oil slick doubles in size every day, so that within fourteen days it has covered the whole bay.

Question: On what day was the bay half covered?

Helping with reading – "DIAL" an answer

Putting prioritising into practice

All of the skills and techniques covered in this chapter can be used to help your child improve reading, writing and thinking skills. There are many occasions when your child might have to answer questions following the reading of a piece of writing (this sort of exercise was sometimes called "comprehension").

Here's a text-based exercise for your child.

The Golden Ticket

An invitation to take part in a tour of his factory is the prize for anyone who finds a Golden Ticket in one of Willy Wonka's chocolate bars. Poor Charlie Bucket never looks likely to achieve this: his family can barely afford basic food to eat, never mind luxuries such as chocolate. So, when he finds some money in the gutter, he cannot resist the temptation to buy just one bar of chocolate.

Charlie went on wolfing the chocolate. He couldn't stop. And in less than half a minute, the whole thing had disappeared down his throat. He was quite out of breath, but he felt marvellously, extraordinarily happy. He reached out a hand to take the change. Then he paused. His eyes were just above the level of the counter. They were staring at the silver coins lying there. The coins were all five-penny pieces. There were nine of them altogether. Surely it wouldn't matter if he spent just one more ...

"I think," he said quietly, "I think ... I'll have just one more of those chocolate bars. The same kind as before, please."

"Why not?" the fat shopkeeper said, reaching behind him again and taking another Whipple-Scrumptious Fudgemallow Delight from the shelf. He laid it on the counter.

Charlie picked it up and tore off the wrapper ... and suddenly ... from underneath the wrapper ... there came a brilliant flash of gold.

Charlie's heart stood still.

"It's a Golden Ticket!" screamed the shopkeeper, leaping about a foot in the air.

"You've got a Golden Ticket! You've found the last Golden Ticket! Hey, would you believe it. Come and look at this, everybody! The kid's found Wonka's last Golden Ticket! There it is! It's right here in his hands!"

It seemed as though the shopkeeper might be going to have a fit. "In my shop, too!" he yelled. "He found it right here in my own little shop! Somebody call the newspapers quick and let them know! Watch out now, sonny! Don't tear it as you unwrap it! That thing's precious!"

(from Roald Dahl, *Charlie and the Chocolate Factory*)

Now you have read the passage from *Charlie and the Chocolate Factory* by Roald Dahl, it's time for the questions:

Practice questions
1. How do we know Charlie enjoyed the Wonka chocolate bar? (5 marks)
2. Compare Charlie's reaction to finding the Golden Ticket to the shopkeeper's. (5 marks)

It's hard to know where to begin! Practise using the following exercise, summarised by the mnemonic "DIAL", in order to help you to "unpick" the questions. This will help your child understand what the question requires you to do more effectively.

The DIAL technique

- **Details**: What will the answer be about?
- **Instructions**: What do you have to do? List? Compare? Explain?
- **Allocation**: How many marks? How many answers do you have to find?
- **Location**: Where will you find the answer? Use highlighter pens etc.

One of the most common causes of poor exam performance is the failure to read the question effectively and therefore to provide the relevant information for the answer. Look how DIAL can help that process to be more effective. Parents of children at all Key Stages have found this a useful tool for concentrating their child's mind on the question.

Applying DIAL an answer

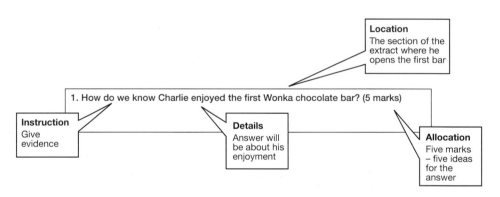

- **Details**: The answer will include evidence that Charlie enjoyed the chocolate bar.
- **Instruction**: We have to show how we know this is true.
- **Allocation:** Five marks means you should try to find five pieces of evidence.
- **Location**: The section of the extract where Charlie opens the first bar.

Now, using a coloured or highlighter pen, go back to the passage from *Charlie and the Chocolate Factory* and mark five relevant pieces of information which show us that Charlie enjoyed the chocolate bar. These will form the basis of the answer.

For example:

- He ate the bar greedily – he "went on wolfing" it.
- He didn't pause while eating it.
- He was breathless with excitement and enjoyment.
- He felt "marvellously, extraordinarily happy".
- He couldn't wait to buy another one.

Now try to answer the second question together. Encourage your child to annotate the question with notes, as the first question was (try using some of the Mind Map® techniques). Here's the question again:

Compare Charlie's reaction on finding the Golden Ticket to the shop-keeper's.

Here's another text to use for practise:

"Mr Gorman" by Garry Burnett

Mr Padley was our headmaster when I started Southcoates Lane Junior Boys' School and I suppose the best way of describing him would be to say that he was like everybody's granddad. He seemed quite old to me, a boy of eight, at the time –the hair had disappeared from the top and back of his head and the sides were always neatly Brylcreemed back. He had a chubby pink face and wore thick glasses that can't have worked very well because he didn't seem to be able to see past the first three rows of the assembly hall. It never seemed to bother him if we swayed in time to the hymn or occasionally when Mr Canon, who played the piano, reminded Whincup, his page turner, to "get a flaming move on". In fact I think he found it all quite funny. And now when I try to think of him I get a picture of Captain Mainwaring from *Dad's Army* in my mind and I'm never sure which is which.

But he always made me feel he cared for the boys in his school, as if they were his own. "*His*" school. I always thought of it as *his* school, the same way I did my house to be *my* house. For some reason I couldn't imagine him anywhere but there and I was shocked out of my skin to see him eating an ice cream on the promenade at Bridlington one day. I almost hid in embarrassment.

When our teacher was off poorly, Mr Padley would sometimes stand in and take the lesson. He was a wonderful story-teller and had a large repertoire of "voices", which he would use to bring them to life. Doing plays was best because he would say, "Who would like to play the part of …?" And before he'd finished everyone's hand would go up. "No one?" he would say, feigning astonishment, "Oh well, I'll have to do that one, then." And he would end up doing every character in the play, each with a different voice, and we would sit back and listen and laugh.

Sometimes in assembly he would read out an article from the newspaper or tell us about somebody who had had something awful happen to them and we would squeeze our eyes shut while he said a special prayer. And I remember the day of the Aberfan disaster in Wales, when a mountain of coal debris slipped and engulfed a tiny school, killing many of its children and teachers, and Mr Padley stood and dabbed his eyes with his handkerchief as he told us all about it in a special assembly before reading a poem to remember the dead. I gave my dinner money to the collection.

So, when Mrs Johnson came in one day to tell us that she had some very sad news and that Mr Padley had died unexpectedly during the night, we all felt the loss as if it were a member of our own family. The shiny black funeral cars drove slowly past the school and we all lined up on Southcoates Lane to sing "For Those in Peril on the Sea", the school hymn, joined by hundreds of ex-pupils and parents. I don't think I'd seen so many people gathered in that way until the Queen came to Hull sometime later. There were lots of people crying.

1. List three things about Mr Padley that you think the boy telling the story found amusing. Give reasons for your choices. (6 marks.)

2. How do we know Mr Padley was a popular teacher? (8 marks.)

Don't forget: DIAL an answer!

Q. 1

D
I
A
L

Q. 2

D
I
A
L

Making comparisons

Spot the difference? There are ten differences between the two cartoons shown overleaf.

Why are comparisons important?

Making comparisons is a normal human activity we do all of the time. For example: "Yesterday's lunch was better than today's"; "I enjoy *Coronation Street* but not *EastEnders*"; "I like pop music but not jazz". Sometimes we make detailed comparisons in order to help us make a decision, perhaps when we are choosing somewhere to go on holiday, buying a new car or deciding where to go for a day out.

Our children are constantly making comparisons, too, and are frequently very skilled at it. All too often comparisons are made without any substantial evidence to support the views they express.

Many assignments, exercises and examination questions invite children to compare ideas, statistics or pieces of writing. The aim of this section is to help you to support and develop your child's ability to make good comparisons.

Start by talking with your child about the word *compare* and also introduce the idea of *contrast*. What's the same and what's different?

What is being compared?

If we are choosing between two different holidays then the criteria for our choice might be based on:

- location
- cost
- climate
- travel arrangements
- places of interest

Things I will learn today

Having a clear set of criteria helps us to make more logical choices and be able to understand *why* those choices have been made. The ability to compare, categorise and identify the similarities and differences between different objects, activities or events *effectively* is an important thinking tool.

Here are some comparing activities:

Choose two television programmes of the same sort, such as soaps, game shows, detective dramas or news programmes. Then identify the similarities and differences between the two programmes.

	Programme 1	Programme 2
Similarities		
Differences		

Here is an example of how you could compare two TV programmes:

	Generation Game	Blind Date
Similarities	Has a game-show host Has an audience Has a prize Shown on Saturday night	Has a game-show host Has an audience Has a prize Shown on Saturday night

Differences	Has a host
	Families compete
	The prizes are objects
	Contestants have to do different
	  kinds of activities
		Has a hostess
		Individuals compete
		The prize is a date
		Contestants have to ask or
		  answer questions

This time make comparisons based on whether or not the objects are *similar*, *different* or *identical* (ask you child to explain what these three words mean). Decide which characteristics you are going to use to compare the objects. Be as clear as possible about *what* it is you are comparing. In other words, what are the *criteria* for comparison? How are they similar? How do they "contrast"? How are they different?

We have started you off with the list for the car and the bicycle.

Objects and criteria	Similar? (Y/N)	Different? (Y/N)	Identical? (Y/N)
Car and bicycle			
Cost?			
Purpose?			
Environment?			
Apple and orange			
Cow and dog			

There are all sorts of opportunities for exercising comparative thinking skills in everyday situations around the home. For example, you might compare cover versions of songs, different books by the same author, or days out in the school holidays.

Using problem solving skills in different situations

Shopping lists

When you are out and about with your child, there are lots of opportunities to practice thinking skills.

At home, ask your child to sort the following list into groups or "sets" and give a name to the categories (dairy produce for example):

Eggs, cereal, chocolate biscuits, milk, yoghurt, potatoes, apples, cheddar cheese, dog biscuits, cat meat, pork sausages, cornflakes, toilet rolls, dishcloth, tights, wine, fish fingers, crab sticks, digestive biscuits, nappies, butter, jam, cream crackers, onions, lettuce, tomatoes, margarine, hamburgers, washing powder, dishwasher tablets, furniture polish, chicken drumsticks, baked beans, croissants.

Before your next visit to the supermarket, ask your child to draw a map of it – which items can be found in which aisle. Ask him to mark where the different foods on your list might be found in the store. Which categories of food are on the map and are not to be found on your shopping list?

At the library

Books in public libraries are organised into categories.

Take your children to the local library and ask them to draw a map of the library according to how the books are categorised. Discuss with them why they think books are organised that way.

Non-fiction books are frequently organised by a system called the Dewey Decimal System. This is a numerical system. Go to the library and find out how it works. Ask the librarian if you need help. Find out the

Dewey Decimal System numbers for yours and your child's favourite topics. Here are some examples to try out:

- pets
- dogs
- rabbits
- transport
- cars
- bikes
- history
- Ancient Rome
- World War One

In the home

Encourage your child to organise your...

- bookshelves
- CDs
- videos/DVDs
- family photographs
- household administration (bills/letters etc.)

Help your child to come up with systems for categorisation and organisation – our CDs were changed around and organised by colour, until we discovered how impractical this system was, and changed to a 'by title' system. It's good to try out ideas and see what works and what does not work (unless you really want to find a CD in a hurry!)

Try to transfer the ideas in this chapter to your child's schoolwork. Organisation and categorisation can help with understanding how ideas connect together in different subjects. What is learned in one subject can support understanding in another, for example Geography and History or Science and RE. Encourage your child to think about using techniques learned in one subject to complete assignments in another – experiment with what works best!

Chapter 9

Memory and Recall

Why is memory important?

In this chapter we will be exploring your child's greatest natural asset to learning – *memory*. We will look at how it works and some of the ways you can make it work even better. All the activities that follow are for you to try out with your child. The 'you' is as much for *you* as for them – give them a try!

You will get some ideas about why we forget things and some hints on how to make this occur less frequently. Contrary to popular opinion, we nearly all have perfect memories already. We may occasionally need to improve our ability to recall, but there is not likely to be much wrong with our memories themselves.

You will find that developing your memory helps with everyday activities, for example shopping. More importantly, it will help your child with important things such as examinations. By learning how to use important memory strategies, you can enhance your recall and accelerate your ability to learn and remember.

Developing and using your memory helps you to see the whole picture (to think holistically), to organise information and make connections between different ideas. A side-effect of improving memory skills is to increase creativity, and, of course, people who are very creative thinkers often go on to be successful in whatever their chosen profession.

Memory types

Memories generally come in one of three categories:

- Incidents, episodes and stories
- Words, objects and names
- Tasks, skills and understanding how to do things

How good do you think your memory is?

First, respond to the statements below as honestly as you can.

- I find it difficult to remember the correct equipment for my children each day at school.　　　　true/not true

- I find it difficult to remember routes and maps.　　　　true/not true

- I find it hard to remember the names of my favourite film stars.　　　　true/not true

- I find it hard to remember the names of famous people from history.　　　　true/not true

- I find it hard to remember how many days there are in each month.　　　　true/not true

- I find spelling some words difficult.　　　　true/not true

- I do not think it is possible to improve your memory.　　　　true/not true

- We remember every single event in our lives.　　　　true/not true

- I can improve my memory and have some fun as well.　　　　true/not true

- If my memory was good, it would help me to be a better learner.　　　　true/not true

Now ask your child to answer the same questions and discuss how each of you responded.

Most people would agree that having a good memory is important for learning, but many of us do not believe that it is possible to do much about improving our memories. This is certainly not the case, as you will see. There are ways to improve your memory and to have fun as well.

Some frequently asked questions about memory

Can we improve our memories?

Definitely *yes*! As you will find in this book, there is nothing to stop us all from developing our memories and recall.

Is every single event that has ever happened in our lives stored somewhere in our brains?

Some scientists believe that it is. We store away every single sight, sound, smell and experience that has happened to us since we were born, and many from *before* we were born! The problem is *recall* – we just can't remember it all.

Is memory really more powerful than a computer?

Yes, and, what is more, our memories are quicker than a computer – when we learn how to use them.

Can improving memory be easy and fun?

It can be if you know how to do it. Improving your memory need not be boring or hard work. It can be fun and can help you to feel much more confident about yourself.

If my child's memory were better, would they learn more?

Almost certainly *yes*! Most of the new subjects your child will learn at secondary school will ask them to use their memory. It might be to remember a list of events in history lessons, some new words in languages classes or a formula in science. The better your child's memory, the easier it will be for them to learn in these subjects.

Does having a good memory mean you are more intelligent?

Not on its own. Having a good memory is just one thinking skill an intelligent person will use. There are extraordinary people with an autistic condition called "savant syndrome", who have incredible memories but who find it difficult to cope with the routines and emotions of everyday life. Being "flexible" with the information is a more effective way of demonstrating you are intelligent. This means being able to *transfer* the thinking about what you have learned into other situations.

In his book *Wise-Up*, Guy Claxton (a Professor at Bristol University) writes about the amazing ability to memorise lines possessed by the actor Anthony Hopkins. Apparently, while filming Stephen Spielberg's *Amistad*, he was able to remember seven pages of lines without a break and to get them right first time when he was filmed. But this is not an ability that he was born with: Hopkins has learned how to use his memory effectively. He has *learned to learn*. This is how Claxton says he does it:

He reads each line over three hundred times, annotating the script with the number of times he has read the section so far. As his recall improves he makes a cross in the margin, then a star out of the cross, and then puts a ring around the star. The script is covered with hand-drawn images, executed in multi-coloured felt-tip; land-scapes, faces, incidents ranging from the Gothic to the futuristic. The lines them-selves are highlighted in green, yellow and blue – orange and red for violent scenes. Hopkins' memory is not an innate talent; it reflects a mastery of learning.

How can you start to improve your memory? Here are some exercises to help you understand that process.

Look carefully at the following twenty objects. After thirty seconds, turn the page and complete the exercise which accompanies them.

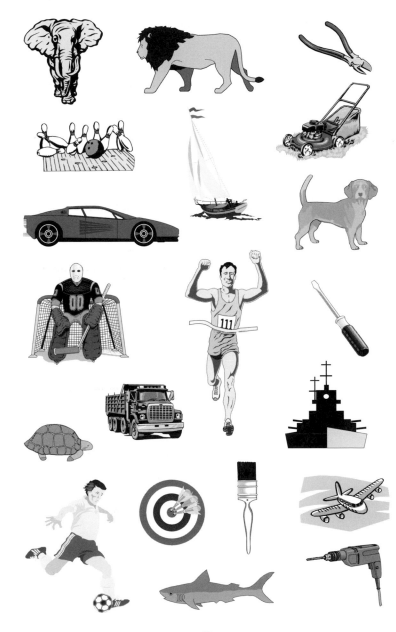

Memory skills – answer sheet

Now try to list as many of the twenty items as you can:

1 _____

2 _____

3 _____

4 _____

5 _____

6 _____

7 _____

8 _____

9 _____

10 _____

11 _____

12 _____

13 _____

14 _____

15 _____

16 _____

17 _____

18 _____

19 _____

20 _____

Now turn back to the illustration sheet of objects and tick the ones that you remembered correctly.

- If you scored 16 to 20, you already have a very good memory and should be looking for ways of making your memory excellent.
- If you scored 11 to 15, your memory is about average, but not nearly as good as it could be.
- If you scored 0 to 10, you will find the work we are going to do in this book really useful and your memory will be much improved by the end of the Chapter.

Test yourself again on the twenty items following the work you are now about to do, in order to see what a difference it can make.

Reflection

One of the ways that we become better learners is by thinking about the *way* we learned something to see how successful it was.

- How did we try to remember these things this time?
- What methods did we use?
- Which of the objects was the easiest to remember? Why?

Our *short*-term memory can handle between 5 and 9 items at once, unless we do something special with the information. Just staring at them will not make a difference to how well we remember them: we need to process the information in some 'extraordinary' way to make a *long*-term memory.

Memory CAM (Chunking Association Mnemonics)

1. Chunking

One of the easiest methods of improving your memory is to group things together into "categories", "sets" or "chunks". Chunking is a way of working with the brain's natural instinct to search for patterns and order. That is why things are easier to remember when they are mentally filed this way. Researchers estimate that it is easier for us to remember information when it is chunked into seven units (plus or minus two units). Take for example the following numbers:

5 2 3 6 5 1 2 3 1 3 0 2 8 2 4 6 0 6 0 2 0 0 4

If we had to remember those numbers for any reason our instinct would be to automatically search for some kind of pattern in order to record the information in our long-term memories.

Look again at the same numbers:

52 365 12 31 30 28 24 60 60 2004

Can you begin to see a pattern now? The clue is "time" and a "year".

If you look back at the twenty items on the sheet (p. 99) you might guess that the items can be grouped into sets of 5. Ask your child to think carefully about what the titles of those groups might be, then try the memory test again using the 'chunking' table below:

Category	Objects				

Is your child trying to learn or revise by looking at an unmanageable whole rather than bite-size chunks? Break down material into more memorable smaller sets.

2. Association

As you will have gathered from our earlier discussion about the structure of the brain and its many interconnections, the neo-cortex (sometimes called the "association cortex") is constantly looking for opportunities to connect information and link it to other networks of meaning. Association means to link together.

Emotion is a very important ingredient in the creation of powerful long-term memories. Lots of people can remember precisely where they were when they heard of Princess Diana's death for example. Sometimes we can "hook" an important piece of information through a visual, auditory or kinaesthetic learning technique and hence record it very powerfully. A very powerful form of association is to link the information to an action or gesture. The more associations you can make, the more likely you are to remember.

Take this example of counting to ten in German:

FIRST THE *TRADITIONAL* WAY – **READ** THE WORDS AND TRY TO REMEMBER THEM

Number	German
1	eins
2	zwei
3	drei
4	vier
5	fünf
6	sechs
7	sieben
8	acht
9	neun
10	zehn

NOW ADD SOME **"AUDITORY"** INFORMATION – SAY THE WORDS ALOUD AS YOU READ THEM

eins   (pronounced eye-ns)
zwei   (pronounced sv-eye)

drei	(pronounced dry)
vier	(pronounced fear)
fünf	(pronounced foonf)
sechs	(pronounced sex)
sieben	(pronounced see ben)
acht	(pronounced act)
neun	(pronounced noyn)
zehn	(pronounced sane)

NOW ADD SOME **"KINAESTHETIC"** INFORMATION – GESTURE

eins	(eyens)	(point to eyes)
zwei	(sveye)	(spy with binoculars)
drei	(dry)	(rub your arm dry)
vier	(fear)	(be frightened)
fünf	(foonf)	(punch)
sechs	(sex)	(wolf-whistle)
sieben	(see ben)	(look for a boy called Ben)
acht	(act)	(perform dramatic gesture)
neun	(noyn)	(think of 'boinging', on springs)
zehn	(sane)	(make a speech bubble, "saying")

Practise this until you can recite the numbers confidently. Associating the action with the word will make very powerful connections and enable you to recall the information in a different way. Now try learning other information in the same way: counting in French, Spanish or whichever language your child is studying, for instance, or remembering a string of historical information or some mathematical or scientific knowledge.

Peg systems
These are another form of association, which work when you connect the information you wish to learn with another object and gesture. The pegs in this system are taken from the children's rhyme "This Old Man": "This old man, he played one, he played knick-knack on my 'drum' ..." and so on. It is likely to appeal to young people, although peg systems are used to great effect by memory experts all around the world.

Number	Peg	Gesture
1	drum	play the drums
2	shoe	tap your foot
3	knee	rub your knee
4	door	knock on the door
5	hive	wave away the bees
6	sticks	point your stick
7	heaven	(heaven) say a prayer
8	gate	open the gate
9	line	peg out the washing on the line
10	hen	feed the chickens

Practise singing and making the gestures with your child until he can confidently go through the full system without a mistake. The important thing is to let the pegs *suggest* the information to you. Making the association can be great fun, the more bizarre, emotional and therefore "memorable" the better.

Practise using the peg system with your child on the following information:

- Sports kit
- After school activities
- The school timetable

Things to remember:

Trainers	Tap foot
Towel	Rub my feet
Packed lunch	Drum my lunch box
Bus fare	Wave away crowds
Pencil case	Point pencil/stick
English book	Knock on English classroom
Homework	Say prayer

3. *Mnemonics, jingles and rhymes*

What does each of the following mnemonics, jingles and rhymes teach us?

*   Never Eat Shredded Wheat
*   In fourteen hundred and ninety-two Columbus sailed the ocean blue
*   Every Good Boy Deserves Favour
*   Richard Of York Gave Battle In Vain
*   Thirty days hath September, April, June and November; all the rest have thirty-one, except February alone which has twenty-eight days clear and twenty nine each leap year.

This kind of language 'play' can be a very powerful way of remembering and uses linguistic and musical intelligence to reinforce the learning.

"**N**ever **E**at **C**ake: **E**at **S**alad **S**andwiches **A**nd **R**emain **Y**oung" is a very useful way of remembering how many c's and s's there are in the word "necessary". Two **S**ausages and one **C**hip is another or one **C**up and two **S**ugars.

> Think up some other mnemonics, jingles or rhymes for facts that your child has found difficult to remember. Your child could make them into posters for her bedroom wall. Devise mnemonics for key information she has learned in a particular subject, or needs to revise for a test.

Story mnemonics
A powerful mnemonic technique for making links and associations is to create a story with strong pictures or images. For example, let us say you want to remember the following shopping list:

*   bread
*   milk
*   cat food
*   wine

You could use this little story: "If you feed hedgehogs on bread and milk then they will be sick. Give them cat food and you drink the wine."

Practise this technique the next time you take your child to the shops. Ask your child to make up a shopping list story, and try not to look at the list at all.

Tony Buzan uses the following story to help remember the order of the planets from Mercury to Pluto (emphasis is author's own).

> One day, the **Sun** was so hot that the **Mercury** in my old-fashioned thermometer burst, burning the leg of the beautiful goddess **Venus**, who fled to **Earth** in pain, only to bump into the god **Mars**, who was burying chocolate bars in the ground. At that moment a Jew called Peter (**Jupiter**) came along wearing a T-shirt with **SUN** on it (**Saturn, Uranus, Neptune**) and walking a dog called **Pluto**.

Try to learn the story and practise on each other. Here is another example to practise:

> **The Seven Dwarfs**
>
> One morning when I woke up I still felt **Sleepy**. I was very **Sneezy** and feeling **Grumpy**, so I thought I had better go to see the **Doc**. "Don't be **Bashful**" she said, "Take off all of your clothes and stand over there." After a quick examination she said, "There is absolutely nothing wrong with you." I felt **Dopey** but **Happy** that the whole thing was over.

Make up some similar mnemonics or story mnemonics with your child for other things that he may need to remember (facts or formulae in maths or science, facts and events in history or other key pieces of information). Remember, the story, and not the list of objects, should be recited. Hopefully the association will trigger the memory effectively.

Key principles of making a strong memory

If you are able to, incorporate some of the following elements into memorising.

Use the chunking, association and mnemonic to configure the material.

Use all your senses
If you use all of your senses and describe what you saw, heard, felt, touched and smelled, then you will probably remember a lot more. Using all of the senses makes the story become more vivid.

Use movement
Actions and gestures are very effective ways of hooking memories and creating kinaesthetic associations.

Use humour
If you have fun with your memory and use funny, ridiculous, rude or surreal images, then you will be more likely to remember them. This is because of the close connection between the limbic centre of the brain, which forms long-term memories, and the generation of strong emotions.

Use symbols
Your subconscious is very good at remembering symbols. In Mindmaps®, especially, the use of symbols such as a lion for courage or a light bulb for a bright idea will cause you to try actively to interpret the symbol and remember it more vividly.

Use colour
The use of colour (coloured highlighter pens or colour coding, for instance) will help to cement the memory visually in your mind.

Use positive images
Our brains are better at remembering positive and pleasant images than negative ones. Some negative images – for example, violent ones – are blocked by the brain.

Exaggeration
Making things bigger, brighter and louder will aid the formation of powerful long-term memories.

Putting it all into practice

Monopoly®⁴ challenge – Take 1

Try to write in (from memory) as many of the properties and places on the London version of the Monopoly® board as you can.

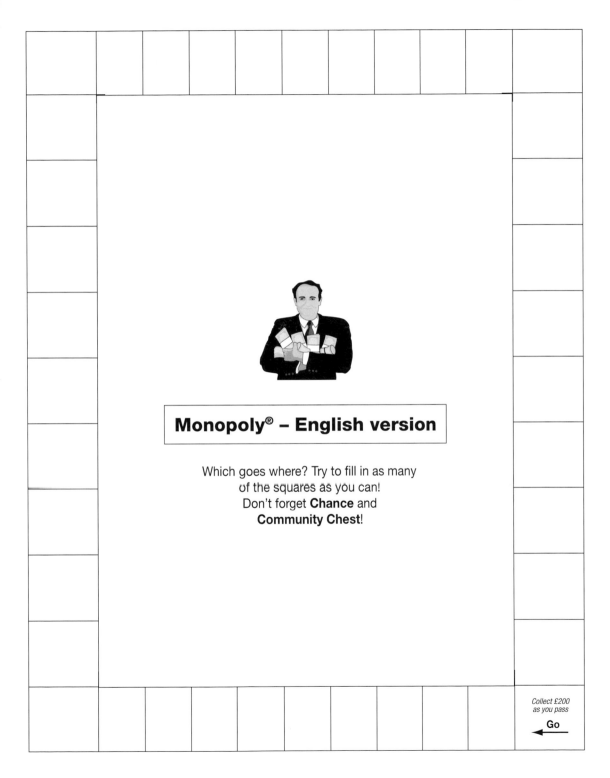

Monopoly® – English version

Which goes where? Try to fill in as many
of the squares as you can!
Don't forget **Chance** and
Community Chest!

*Collect £200
as you pass*

Go

Free parking	The Strand	? Chance	Fleet Street	Trafalgar Square	*Fenchurch Street Station*	Leicester Square	Coventry Street	Water Works	Piccadilly	Go to jail
Vine Street										Regent Street
Marlborough Street										Oxford Street
Community Chest										Community Chest
Bow Street										Bond Street
Marylebone Station										*Liverpool Street Station*
Northumberland Avenue										? Chance
Whitehall										Park Lane
Electric Company										Super Tax
Pall Mall										Mayfair
Jail	Penton-ville Road	Euston Road	? Chance	The Angel Islington	*Kings Cross Station*	Income tax	White-chapel Road	Community Chest	Old Kent Road	Go ←

Monopoly® – English version

Answer sheet

Reflecting on the way you learned

How did you try to remember the order of the spaces? Did you ...

- use visual reference points (colour, illustrations etc.)?
- give "value" to the colours, such as "rich royal blues", "dirty browns"?
- attach some personal or emotional significance to the properties ("I always go for the greens because ...")?
- use kinaesthetic reference points (by trying to imagine you were playing)?
- plot the corners and the stations in a logical mathematical way?
- use some other ingenious method?

The way you went about the task might tell you something about your preferred style of learning and remembering.

Monopoly® challenge – Take 2

Now, using chunking, association and mnemonic memory methods, devise a way of remembering all of the properties and stations in the correct order. Test each other!

The true value of an exercise like this is of course in the "transfer".

Can you think of other situations where you might need to remember lots of objects or information or objects in the correct order?

Spelling, for example, is one area where these techniques might be used. We will look at this area next.

---

[4] Monopoly®, the distinctive design of the game board and the four corner squares are registered trademarks of Hasbro, Inc.

Chapter 10

Help Your Child to Learn to Spell

"Christopher Robin respects Owl, because you can't help respecting someone who can spell Tuesday, even if he doesn't spell it right, but spelling isn't everything. There are days when spelling Tuesday simply doesn't count."

The House at Pooh Corner, **AA Milne**

Although Christopher Robin is quite right, that there is a lot more to the successful and effective use of language than just being able to spell words correctly, spelling is an important skill because it enables your child to communicate meaning clearly in writing.

There are lots of complicated new words your child will be expected to learn at all stages of her education – far too many to write down here. The aim, therefore, is to develop an effective way of learning new spellings that she can use with any word she meets, in any subject.

The work you did in Chapter 9 will now be put to the test. Remember to use the very powerful ways of working with your brain and all of your intelligences to learn. Encourage your child at every stage, and praise successes at every opportunity, however modest.

How to learn to learn to spell

Try using the following approaches to help your child with learning spellings in the future.

Step 1: Look at how the word has been attempted

Which part of the word does your child need to learn? If your child misspells a word, look carefully at the parts of the word spelled correctly, and the parts of the word misspelled this time. Affirm that she will always spell the word correctly in the future and that the mistake was a mere temporary "setback". Congratulate her for the letters she did get in the correct place and order.

Step 2: Actions

1. *Chunking*
*   Take a word such as "caterpillar": how many words can you see inside it? (Cat, pill, pillar, ill, at, ate, cater.) So, "My cat ate a pill and was ill behind a **pillar**. I cannot **cater** for her!"
*   Take the word "friend" (a fri**end** will always be there in the **end**)
*   Remember "sep**arate**" has a **rat** in it!
*   Imagine **abundance** (plenty) as **a bun dance**

Make a list of twenty words that have *other words* inside them. Write the "other" words in a different colour:

*   Safeway (*safe, few, way*)
*   Manchester (*man, chest*)
*   Scarborough (*scar, car, rough*)

Then make up a "silly sentence" with each of the "found words" in – for example, "I always feel very **SAFE** when I'm shopping in Safeway!"

2. *Association*
Earlier, we saw that learning to count in German could be supported by associating the word with a physical action, in order for it to be encoded onto our long-term memory systems. As you know, this kind of "connecting" to something else is very effective because it works with the brain's natural way of linking information to other knowledge.

Take the word "shoe", which doesn't look much like it sounds (shoo). If your child wanted to learn to spell "shoe", one way he could learn it by association would be to connect it to words he can already spell with an identical letter string. For example: sh**oe**, t**oe**, f**oe**, h**oe**, d**oe**s.

"I nearly lost my **toe** when a **foe** took a **hoe** and chopped my **shoe**. What **does** he think he's doing?"

Remember, you may h**ear** with your **ear**.

You could link a word such as "lau**gh**ter" with fi**ght**, ti**ght**, mi**ght** and si**ght**.

Find words you can associate with each of the following:

here	**dis**appear	**sch**ool	sensi**ble**
there	dis	sch	ible
where	dis	sch	ible

3.   Mnemonics, jingles and rhymes
Using emotion (humour or surprise, for instance) can help create powerful memories. Take a word such as "beautiful", which has what could be a tricky beginning: "beau". If you were to make a mnemonic like "**b**ad **e**ggs **a**re **u**seless", it can help you to remember the order of that letter string.

Think of some "fun" mnemonics, jingles or rhymes with your child that will be useful for remembering spellings. Ask your child to design a poster which will help teach someone how to spell a new word. A cartoon illustration will help bring the idea to life!

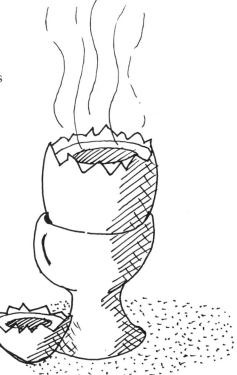

115

Step 3: *Show you know*

- **Cover** the word from view; try to see it on the inside of your eyelids
- **Say** the word aloud
- **Write** the word down
- **Check** it and
- **Repeat** the process – the more repetitions the better!

Practise this short dictation on each other:

"I bought a turquoise ukulele from a character outside the stationery shop adjacent to the Coliseum. I frequently give recitals of medieval compositions in Vienna."

Devise some different ways of learning the words so you can spell them all correctly. Once your child has learned to learn to spell he can apply these techniques to any new learning situation (and so can you!).

Multiply your score by 4 to give a percentage. Test yourselves and see how quickly you can improve your score.

Here are some examples of how to learn to spell words in the practice dictation using "Learning to Learn" memory techniques:

1. Chunking

Character	**Char act er**
Medieval	**Me die val**
Adjacent	**Adj ace cent**
Compositions	**Compo position sit**

2. Association

Stationery	Paper
Frequently	Frequent**ly fly**
Recitals	**Vital** recital
Coliseum	**Col**in goes to the mu**seum**

3. Mnemonics

Uncle
Kevin
Usually
Likes
Eating
Larks
Eggs

"**U K U L E L E**"

Chapter 11

Summary – Making Learning Effective

Colin Rose is an internationally renowned expert on learning and the brain. He explains that effective revision and learning will not always happen "by chance" and that it is possible to make the whole process more effective by following a pattern which puts into practice all of the learning-to-learn theories we have explored in this book.

Before you begin, visualise the outcome (look ahead to what will be the outcome of learning this new skill or piece of information). Encourage your child to experiment with visualisations – imagining the successful and positive outcome of his efforts and studies.

Stage 1: Preparation – the frame of mind

Always have a very positive outlook about your prospects and abilities. Tell yourself and your children that you *can* do well!

Find an appropriate place to work. This should be warm, quiet and comfortable. Take regular breaks (try not to work for more than forty minutes at a time). Have a good supply of clear water, which you sip often. Move around, oxygenate your brain!

Play relaxing music (choose quiet classical music for studying). Break down your work into smaller chunks, sets or units.

Stage 2: Get the information

Be clear exactly what it is you are learning. Categorise the learning. Is it just "facts" and "knowledge"? Or are you practising a skill that is linked to a higher level than you are currently on? Ask your child's teacher what he needs to *do* with the information he is trying to learn in order to lift his level of attainment. (compare, hypothesise, analyse, etc.).

Get the "big picture" of what your child is studying (read simplified versions, find a synopsis, watch a video, summarise, look at the headlines etc.).

Get the information in a way that suits your learning style (visual, auditory, kinaesthetic). Take your learning-style test to see which best suits you.

Stage 3: Explore the information

Use a combination of intelligences to explore the subject. Imagine there are several pages of information to revise.

Highlight key points using different coloured highlighter pens. Write information on Post-it® notes and place them around the room. Mind-map the topic being revised. Swap Mind Maps® with others.

Record the information onto a cassette. Play it in "dead time" (travelling, queuing etc.) Teach somebody else. Have "study-buddy" evening lessons.

Make mnemonics to summarise the information. Turn information into a "song" or "rap". Use karaoke tapes to help.

Make up quiz questions based on your revision topic. Record the questions onto a cassette and play them back to yourself in "dead time".

Stage 4: Make a "memory"

Make connections between what you have learned and the new information. Sort the information into categories or "chunks". Read it aloud, speak to others, write it down, draw symbols and diagrams.

Use mnemonics, jingles, rhymes. Try to turn the information into "pictures" or "gestures" that can be acted out in an exaggerated way.

Stage 5: Show that you know

Use another person to help demonstrate that the information has been learned (family member, friend, study buddy). Think about *how* you will show you know (write it down, speak, act, draw it etc.).

Stage 6: Think about the whole process

Ask yourself some questions, such as:

*   What could I do better next time?
*   Is there anything I could improve in any way?
*   What else do I need to know?
*   Is there perhaps a different way of doing things I didn't use the first time around?

Conclusion

We hope that this book has helped you to understand *how* you can enhance your own skills, knowledge and experience when helping and supporting your child through their educational development.

The strategies are meant to help you maximise your understanding of teaching and learning styles so you can make learning fun for the family.

We really believe that parents *can* and *will* make a difference to the attainment of their children with positive encouragement, support and praise!

And finally, we wish you all the best in continuing to develop a learning culture in the home that all the family will appreciate and value. Believe in your own and your children's abilities—you *can* make it happen!

Appendix

Finding information together

Parents often feel that they don't have the knowledge to assist their children with their schoolwork because the content has changed so much since their own schooldays. However, you do have many skills and experiences that can assist with reinforcing what they are learning and broaden their experiences.

Go to the library together

A child needs to know that adults don't necessarily know everything and that learning is something we continue to do throughout life. A visit to the library could become a tremendous fun activity to see who can find the most interesting and relevant information. (See Chapter 8 "Thinking Skills".)

Search the Internet together

Even if you don't have access in the home, there are lots of places in the community that offer Internet access, such as adult learning centres. Your local library should be able to find these, or may even have a row of computers for public use, as many libraries now do.

A child will enjoy teaching *you* how to search the Internet, for example! It is good for self-esteem and confidence to be able to teach someone else.

Useful websites
There are hundreds of useful educational websites you might bookmark for your child. Intelligent searches will provide details and links to most topics studied in schools. Here are just a few useful addresses of recommended sites you might like to browse together. These sites themselves

have lots of links and recommended sites that provide rich resources for learning together with your child.

www.learningalive.co.uk – Pathways (top twenty websites),
BT Learning Centre, Living Library

www.northhullclc.com

www.bbc.co.uk/education/ks3bitesize/

www.gridclub.com

www.bonjour.org.uk

www.parentcentre.gov.uk

Places of interest

You could visit places that are linked to topics being studied at school. Museums are becoming increasingly accessible for children as they present relevant interactive activities to provoke thinking about what they are seeing.

When planning a holiday, give some thought to whether certain destinations may be more beneficial educationally than others. A youngster who is studying a foreign language will benefit enormously from listening to and speaking the language she is studying in the country itself, as well as gaining confidence in front of you by speaking on behalf of the family.

Speak to other people

Encourage your child to spend time with and talk with other members of the family and friends. This will both broaden his understanding of others' diverse life experiences and exercise his interpersonal intelligence.

Books, tapes and games

Read books together relating to the subject area and talk about them. Encourage your child to think about and question what he is reading. If he is studying the Victorians, for example you might ask him to compare how children lived then and now. Encourage him to point out the similarities and differences.

Try to have an encyclopaedia, dictionary and atlas in the home for reference. These could be in book form or as software packages on the computer. A child will benefit from being able to access information from a variety of sources.

Again, not only will this engage different learning styles but will also get him thinking more widely about *where* sources of information are available to him.

Music as aid to learning

"Music stimulates the emotional centre of our brain and our emotions are strongly linked to long-term memory. So, playing background music as you learn, especially quiet, classical music, has proved to be effective for many people."

Colin Rose, *Master it Faster* (1999)

For younger children, music and movement can be a very powerful way of helping them to learn. Remember the ABCDEFG song? Or counting songs such as "Five Little Speckled Frogs"?

Based on what you already know and have read so far, how can you continue to develop a learning culture within the home?

To be able to teach, explain or show someone else what you have learned really reinforces your own understanding.

! Remember: Try to make learning fun and interesting.

Glossary

admission authorities:	Authorities who allocate a specific school to a child.
attainment targets:	Targets to determine what children should be expected to know and be able to do by the end of each **key stage** of the **national curriculum**.
baseline assessment:	Assessment of a child's skills and abilities, which is usually carried out by the teachers within the first term of starting school. With this information the teacher can plan lessons and measure the progress of the child. Areas covered include language and literacy, maths and personal and social development.
CAT:	Cognitive-ability test. This gives an indication of a child's potential. These tests are used extensively in secondary schools to predict GCSE results.
catchment area:	Geographical area that surrounds a school. A factor that is often considered by **admission authorities** when deciding which school a child is to attend. (However, parents have a right to express a preference for the school they wish their child to attend regardless of where they live.)
county and controlled schools:	Schools wholly funded by the local education authority (**LEA**).
Department for Education and Skills (DfES):	Central government department that has responsibility for education and employment.
disapplication:	Term used where a pupil is exempt from certain **national-curriculum** requirements. Some pupils with special educational needs may be disapplied, for example, if their disability makes it impossible for them to study some subjects in the national curriculum.
education action zones (EAZs):	Local clusters of schools – usually a mix of not more than twenty primary, secondary and special schools, working in partnership with the **LEA**, local parents, businesses and others. The aim of the partnership is to encourage innovative approaches to raising standards in education.

exclusion:	Suspension of a pupil from school by the teacher, either temporarily or permanently, on disciplinary grounds.
FE:	Further education – college-level education.
GCSE:	General Certificate of Secondary Education, an examination introduced in 1988 to replace GCE O-level and CSE examinations. Usually taken at 16 but brighter children can take them earlier.
GCSE Bitesize:	BBC revision guide that uses TV, books and the Internet to help children to prepare for GCSE examinations.
GNVQ:	General National Vocational Qualification – vocational qualification in work-related subjects taken mainly by pupils who are aged sixteen and in full-time education (SNVQ in Scotland).
HE:	Higher education – university-level education.
home–school agreements:	All state schools are required to have written home–school agreements, drawn up in consultation with parents. They are non-binding statements explaining the school's aims and values, the responsibilities of both school and parents, and what the school expects of its pupils. Parents will be invited to sign a parental declaration, indicating that they understand and accept the contents of the agreement.
ICT:	Information and communications technology.
IEP:	Individual education programme. Programmes that are drawn up by a class teacher and/or special-needs coordinator within a school to provide individual support for children deemed to have needs over and above those of other children in the class.
KS:	Key stage. These relate to the four stages of pupils' progress in acquiring knowledge and skills as set out in the national curriculum. Pupils are tested at the end of each stage. Key stage 1: 3–7 years Key stage 2: 7–11 years Key stage 3: 12–13 years Key stage 4: 14–16 years
LEA:	Local education authority – the body that has responsibility for providing education to pupils of school age in its area.

national curriculum:	Covers what pupils should be taught in state-maintained schools. The national curriculum covers eleven subjects overall and is divided into four **key stages**.
national curriculum levels:	All pupils undergo national tests and teacher assessments at ages seven, eleven and fourteen. The school is required to report to parents what level their child has reached in both tests and teacher assessment.
national numeracy strategy:	Government initiative that aims to raise standards of numeracy.
OFSTED:	Official body that inspects state-funded schools in England. The aim is to improve standards of achievement and quality of education. The equivalents elsewhere in the UK are HMIS (Her Majesty's Inspector of Schools) in Scotland, ESTYN in Wales and Department of Education in Northern Ireland.
prospectus:	Brochure produced by the school containing useful facts and information to enable parents to make comparisons when choosing schools.
PSHE:	Personal, social and health education.
SATs:	Standard assessment tests and tasks – nationally set tests and tasks for pupils at the end of each key stage.
SEN:	Special education needs. This term is used to describe the needs of any child who has been identified as having needs over and above those of others in the class.
SNUTs:	Standard National Tests (KS3 tests).

Answers

Parents' examples of things they have learned successfully:
- Driving
- Cooking
- Being a parent
- Spelling
- DIY

Parents' examples of things they experienced difficulty learning:
- Maths
- Foreign language
- Driving
- Learning lines for a play

Parents' examples of things their child has learned well in the past:
- Walking
- Talking
- Riding a bicycle
- Reading
- Manners

Join the dots

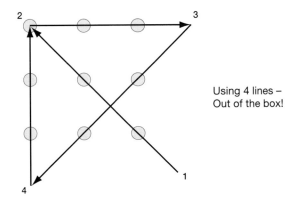

Using 4 lines –
Out of the box!

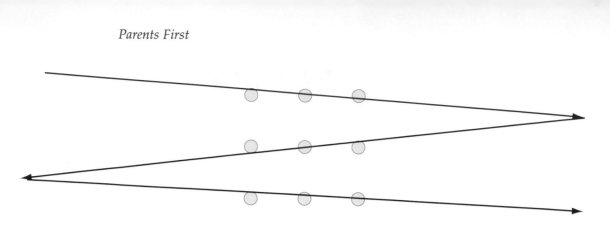

Using 3 lines – A kind of zig-zag

Using 1 line –
A very thick line

Antony and Cleopatra
They were both goldfish.

The hotel detective
The postman was the only man in the room.

Prioritising
1. IIRI
2. IRII
3. RRRR

Further exercises in "sifting" for relevant information
1. None
2. Peahens, not peacocks, lay eggs
3. Day 13 (it doubles in size each day)

Bibliography

Angelou, Maya, 1995, *The Collected Poems of Maya Angelou*, Virago Press, London.

Armstrong, Thomas, 2000, *7 kinds of Smart: Identifying and Developing Your Multiple Intelligences*, Plume Books, London.

Blagg, Nigel, *et al.*, 1988, *Somerset Thinking Skills Course*, Nigel Blagg Associates.

Brearley, Michael, 2001, *Emotional Intelligence in the Classroom*, Crown House Publishing, Carmarthen.

Burnett, Garry, 2002, *Learning to Learn: Making Learning Work for All Students*, Crown House Publishing, Carmarthen, Wales.

Burnett, Garry, 2002, *Learning to Learn: A Video Workpack*, Crown House Publishing, Carmarthen, Wales.

Buzan, Tony, 1989, *Use Your Memory*, BBC Books, London.

Buzan, Tony, 2000, *Head First: Ten Ways to Tap into Your Natural Genius*, Harper Collins, London.

Buzan, Tony, 2001, *The Mind Map Book: Millennium Edition*, BBC Consumer Publishing, London.

Campolo, Tony, 2000, *Let Me Tell You a Story*, "W" Publishing Group, Pennsylvania.

Claxton, G., 2000, *Hare Brain, Tortoise Mind: Why Intelligence Increases When You Think Less*, Ecco Press, New York.

Claxton, G., 2000, *Wise-Up: The Challenge of Lifelong Learning*, Bloomsbury, London.

Crystal, David, 1986, *Listen To Your Child: A Parent's Guide to Children's Language*, Penguin, London.

Dahl, Roald, 1985, *Charlie and the Chocolate Factory*, Puffin Books, London.

DePorter, Bobbie, 1992, *Quantum Learning*, Dell Publishing, New York.

Dryden, Gordon, and Vos, Jeanette, 2001, *The Learning Revolution*, Network Educational Press, Stafford, UK.

Fisher, Robert, 1999, *Head Start: How to Develop Your Child's Mind*, Souvenir Press, London.

Gardner, Howard ([1983 Basic Books] 1993), *Frames of Mind: The Theory of Multiple Intelligences*, Fontana, London.

Gardner, Howard, 1993, *Multiple Intelligences: The Theory in Practice*, Basic Books, Oxford.

Gardner, Howard, 2000, *Intelligence Reframed: Multiple Intelligence For the 21st Century*, Basic Books, Oxford.

Gardner, Howard, 2000, *The Disciplined Mind: Beyond Facts and Standardized Tests*, Penguin Books, New Jersey.

Goleman, Daniel, 1996, *Emotional Intelligence: Why It Matters More Than IQ*, Bloomsbury, London.

Gottman, John, 1997, *The Heart of Parenting: How to raise an Emotionally Intelligent Child*, Bloomsbury, London.

Greenfield, Susan, 1994, *The Royal Institution Christmas Lectures: Journey to the Centre of the Brain*, BBC, London.

Jensen, Eric, 1995, *Brain-Based Learning*, The Brain Store Inc., San Diego, California.

Jensen, Eric, 1997, *Neuro-Tour: A Guide To The Human Brain*, The Brain Store Inc., San Diego, California.

Jensen, Eric, 1998, *Teaching with the Brain in Mind*, Atlantic Books, Tunbridge Wells, Kent.

Knight, S., 1999, *Introducing NLP*, IPD, London.

Laing, J. (ed.), 1994, *Increase Your Learning Power*, Timelife Books (Dorling Kindersley), Amsterdam.

Lazear, David, 1994, *Seven Pathways of Learning: Teaching with Students and Parents about Multiple Intelligences*, Zephyr Press, Tucson, Arizona.

Lindenfield, G., 1994, *Confident Children*, Thorson's (HarperCollins), London.

Lindenfield, G., 1996, *Self Motivation*, Thorson's (HarperCollins), London.

Lucas, Bill, 2001, *Power Up Your Mind: Learn Faster, Work Faster*, Nicholas Brealey Publishing, London.

Mackay, I., 1998, *Listening Skills*, IPD, London.

Mackay, I., 1998, *Asking Questions*, IPD, London.

Mumford, A., 1999, *Effective Learning*, IPD, London.

Rose, Colin, 1992, *Accelerate Your Learning*, Accelerated Learning Systems, Aylesbury, Bucks.

Rose, Colin, 1999, *Master it Faster*, Accelerated Learning Systems, Aylesbury, Bucks.

Rose, Colin, and Nicholl, Malcolm J, 2000, *Accelerated Learning for the Twenty First Century*, Dell Publishing, New York, NY.

Schaffer, R., 1990, *Mothering: The Developing Child*, Fontana Paperbacks, London.

Schaffer, R., 1999, *Developmental Psychology – Childhood to Adolescence*, Brooks/Cole, Pacific Grove.

Sloane, Paul, 1999, *Lateral Thinking Puzzles,* Sterling, New York, NY.

Smith, Alistair, 1996, *Accelerated Learning in the Classroom*, Network Educational Press, Stafford.

Smith, P. K., Cowlie, H. and Blades, M., 1998, *Understanding Children's Development*, Blackwell Publishers, Oxford.

Strong, Julia, 1999, *Writing Frames: Whole School Approach to Literacy*, HarperCollins, London.

Tice, Lou, 1989, *Investment in Excellence*, The Pacific Institute, Seattle.

Tice, Lou, 1991, *Strategic Thinking for Strategic Planning*, The Pacific Institute, Seattle.

Treffert, Darrold A., 1989, *Extraordinary People*, Black Swan Publishing, London.

USA & Canada *orders to:*
Crown House Publishing
P.O. Box 2223, Williston, VT 05495-2223, USA
Tel: 877-925-1213, Fax: 802-864-7626
www.CHPUS.com

UK & Rest of World *orders to:*
The Anglo American Book Company Ltd.
Crown Buildings, Bancyfelin, Carmarthen, Wales SA33 5ND
Tel: +44 (0)1267 211880/211886, Fax: +44 (0)1267 211882
E-mail: books@anglo-american.co.uk
www.anglo-american.co.uk

Australasia *orders to:*
Footprint Books Pty Ltd.
Unit 4/92A Mona Vale Road, Mona Vale NSW 2103, Australia
Tel: +61 (0) 2 9997 3973, Fax: +61 (0) 2 9997 3185
E-mail: info@footprint.com.au
www.footprint.com.au

Singapore *orders to:*
Publishers Marketing Services Pte Ltd.
10-C Jalan Ampas #07-01
Ho Seng Lee Flatted Warehouse, Singapore 329513
Tel: +65 6256 5166, Fax: +65 6253 0008
E-mail: info@pms.com.sg
www.pms.com.sg

Malaysia *orders to:*
Publishers Marketing Services Pte Ltd
Unit 509, Block E, Phileo Damansara 1, Jalan 16/11
46350 Petaling Jaya, Selangor, Malaysia
Tel : 03 7955 3588, Fax : 03 7955 3017
E-mail: pmsmal@po.jaring.my

South Africa *orders to:*
Everybody's Books
Box 201321 Durban North 401, 1 Highdale Road,
25 Glen Park, Glen Anil 4051, KwaZulu NATAL, South Africa
Tel: +27 (0) 31 569 2229, Fax: +27 (0) 31 569 2234
E-mail: ebbooks@iafrica.com